Teach Me Your Way, Oh Lord

Teach Me Your Way, Oh Lord

A Glimpse of My Past and
Six Different Views of My Present

Victoria R. Bradley

> **NOTE:** The sale of this book without its cover is unauthorized. If you purchased this book without a cover, you should be aware that it was reported to the publisher as "unsold and destroyed." Neither the author nor the publisher has received payments for the sale of this stripped book.

DBEM Publishing
Columbia, SC 29223

Teach Me Your Way, Oh Lord

Copyright © 2022 by Victoria R. Bradley

All rights reserved

No portion of this book may be reproduced, stored in a retrieval system, or transmitted in any form by any means–electronic, mechanical, photocopy, recording, or other–except for brief quotations in printed reviews, without prior permission of the author.

ISBN: 978-1-7358061-1-2
Printed in the United States

Second Edition

Contents

The Beginning of My Journey	Pages 1-20
Master's Degree	Pages 21-43
Re: Let's Do It Again	Pages 44-65
The Body	Pages 66-154
The Weather of Your Life	Pages 155-167
Thorns Among Roses	Pages 168-196
I Want to Be a Cover Girl	Pages 197-220

Dedication

To: My Father God *(First and Foremost)*

Lord, I could not have written these lessons if you had not taught me through others and inspired me to do so. I thank you for teaching me and I thank you for those you sent to help me along my life's journey…they, like you, have loved me in spite of me.

Acknowledgements

I would like to acknowledge the people below who have impacted my life in so many ways. Thank you all.

My Children	Jerrod
	Cecil, Jr.
	Sheila
My "Jonathans"	Gloria
	Eleanor
	Jackie
	Debra
	Mary
	Donna
	Priscilla

I would like to also acknowledge my deceased family members and friends who equally impacted my life:

My Mother	Barbara Pierce
My Father	Frazier Mitchell
My Grandmother	Mary Ragins
My Grandfather	James Ragins
My Great Grandmother	Sena Ragins
My Great Grandfather	Charlie Ragins
My Sister	Kellie Murray
My Aunt	Martha Mitchell
My Friends	Evelyn Boykin
	Patricia Moore

Words by the Author

Children, I can tell you that it has been quite a journey, and it's not over yet. When I've felt alone, I now know that I was not alone. I was being tested and carried. I was being prepared and processed for what was to come. At times, I could not see the reasons for all the "stuff" that took place in my life, but I can truly thank God for orchestrating my trip.

I've made some bad choices and decisions, and I've been often disobedient, but God, being so gracious and so merciful has taught me and has forgiven me because I repented. He has kept me for such a time as this.

When I penned the glimpse of my past, I wondered why He led me to write about the past when He was speaking so profoundly of the NOW. Well, there has to be a past before there can be a present or a future. As I continue on my journey, you will be able to continue with me because you will know from whence I came.

God, Be Glorified!!!

The Beginning of My Journey

A Glimpse of My Past

Victoria R. Bradley

THE BEGINNING OF MY JOURNEY

A Glimpse of My Past

These few pages, by no means, cover all of my life. These are only a few pieces the Father (God) has allowed me to share with you. Most people in this life haven't a clue about this life. Each of us is on a journey back to God. We have different assignments on our journey. We go from place to place, job to job, church to church and never realize that these moves are assignments that were ordained for us before we were ever born. (Ephesians 1:4-6)

All the specifics that took place in my life as I grew up at one time seemed so important by themselves. The only importance I have come to understand is the fact that I learned from these things – the good and the bad. I might add that I am not one of the fastest learners either. I thank God that we that love him know that all things work together for our good and His purpose. (Romans 8:28)

We have choices to make. There are signs everywhere. Some time we read the signs, sometimes we miss the signs, some time we misinterpret the signs, and some time we ignore the signs. Then, we come to forks or dead ends and don't know which way to go. We may go the wrong way, only wasting time because we must return to the starting place and begin again. We must learn from the mistakes or we will continue in circles. Before we realize it, many years have passed and we have not reached our destiny. We do have a purpose to live out – we are not here just to exist.

Realizing who we are and whose we are is one of the most important truths we could ever learn. If we understand that, we will go from faith to faith and glory to glory.

(2 Corinthians 3:18/Romans 1:17/Jeremiah 1:5; 29:11)

We all come from different walks of life…we can choose to let the circumstances, situations, and conditions of life keep us in bondage or we can choose to learn from them and be free as we travel. All of us have sinned and fallen short of God's glory (no one exempt). We all need the same thing – salvation.

Within these pages, I went from "seeking other things first and seeking the Lord last" to "seeking Him first and allow all other things to be added to me." (Matthew 6:33)
I also left off from being a "Martha" and am now a "Mary." (Luke 10:38-42) and the Lord gave me some wonderful "Jonathans" along the way.

I was born on December 12, 1952, a few months ahead of my scheduled time, weighing almost 2 pounds. I was incubated for 31 days and was not expected to live. I survived and now I get to share some of my life's history.

I grew up on Longland Plantation in Williamsburg County, South Carolina, at a time and place of farming.

Growing up in the country was quite an experience.

- We always had something to pick: beans, peas, corn, cucumbers (vegetables for sale and consumption); cotton and tobacco (other income)

- We always had animals to feed - dogs, hogs, chickens, and cats.

- We always had chores to do.

Work outside the house consisted of hoeing, sweeping or raking the yard; gathering fire wood; washing clothes, and whatever else you were told to do. Let me tell you about washing clothes. We used a pail to fill the machine with water for washing and then filled two large tubs with water for rinsing. We had no inside water – only an outside pump and it was situated in the yard.

Work inside the house consisted of cooking, cleaning, dusting, and mopping and waxing our linoleum floors. We enjoyed the waxing because we got to buff the floors by putting on thick wool socks and sliding across the floors. Washing, drying, and putting away the dishes after every meal was a must in our house – we were the dish washer. It was also our job to make sure we had two pails filled with water in the kitchen before night came.

My grandmother was the backbone of our family...it seemed like her work was never done. She was truly God-sent. She taught me many things to which I am so thankful. She made sure that I knew how to sew, how to iron, how to make the beds, and do it with excellence. My grandmother worked at the big house, came from the job and worked some more. She made delicious meals on a wood stove. She gathered firewood and would be up early to start the fire so the house would be warm when the rest of the family got up. You would think my grandfather would be the one to do this but he never covered my grandmother as the man of the house or us kids. She made, repaired, washed, and ironed clothes, and always found time to keep my hair washed, oiled and braided. I could go on and on and still not be able to list all of the things she did to make our lives better. I never understood where she found the time and energy to do it all. She was such a blessing.

My grandfather, on the other hand, worked in the fields, but after he came home from the job that was it. He acted like the king with maids to order. I didn't care very much for him because of his drinking. He would often fight my grandmother when he came home and I didn't care to spend time around him.

My grandmother and I spent many precious moments together on the front porch. We had a swing on the porch that hung from the ceiling. It was something about swinging on cool nights and also after rain showers. There was a highway in front of the house and we would watch the cars and trucks go by and watch lightning bugs fly around.

We enjoyed listening to gospel music and sermons by Reverend R.W. Schambach on the radio as we sat in the swing talking and enjoying the cool of the evenings. At those times, you could sleep with the doors open and the windows up. The cool breeze would flow throughout the house.

At certain times each year (I don't remember what months), the women in the neighborhood would gather at each other's' homes to make quilts by hand. I enjoyed watching them and remember being quite excited about the finished product. I still have a few of those quilts to this day.

There were days growing up in the country that I wished to escape, like the days we made lye (octagon) soap in the black wash pot or the days when we killed pigs. These were "all day" affairs. We killed at least one pig every year and spent the entire day processing it – preparing sections for freezing, for curing, and making sausages and cheeses.

We were quite healthy growing up. The old-time remedies worked (and still do). The tallow (made from fat) for the chest colds; the sassafras tea for the throat; the castor and/or cod liver oil for worms; the homemade concoctions (asafetida granules, liquor, garlic, onion and whatever else) for stomach problems; fat back and sardine for the mumps, and on and on. They all worked, believe it or not.

Going to church was a must – it was never up for discussion. We went almost every Sunday and always in time for Sunday school too. We had a car but my grandfather almost always managed to come home after we were almost at church (walking), after we had walked back from church, or he didn't come at all.

As far as education went, I enjoyed school and looked forward to each day. Listed below are some of my fondest memories of elementary school.

- Singing songs like *Old McDonald, Early in the Morning, Bring Back My Bunny to Me, The Mulberry Bush, Shake it Up-Shake it Down, Heal-Toe 123, and the Bunny Hop.*

- The school lunches were delicious; the cheese slices and the biscuits were my favorite parts of the meal.
- My first notebook - my notebook had the brand name of VICTORY on the front of it and for my first year of school, I thought it was nice of them to have my name printed on my notebook. How could one confuse VICTORY with VICTORIA?

- The sweet smell of the rubbing alcohol that was used in the health room when students had a bruise or a fever

- A "not so fond" but vivid remembrance was a girl named "Ada" that sat next to me in first grade and stole my lunch. I was just waiting for recess so I could eat my syrup cornbread muffins and they were gone.

- The many enjoyable activities on April-Fools Day and May Day

- My 4th grade teacher (Ms. Sadie). She had a way of pinching with a twist, when you acted up in class or in the hallways

- A cousin named Patricia who told us that they had a cow that gave chocolate milk, and we believed her

- A boy who always followed me around asking if he could carry my books and my answer was always "NO"

- A boy who transferred to our school in 8th grade whom I fell in love with

When I was in 6th grade, I found out that I needed glasses. Up until that time, I thought that I was seeing everything that everyone else was seeing. One day the teacher called on me to fill in a sentence on the blackboard and I could not see it. She asked, "Can't you see that from your seat?" and I told her that I could not. She sent me to the nurse who checked my eyes and made an appointment for me to have more testing done. I was told that I was nearsighted. A few weeks later I had glasses – Wow, what a difference.

When we transferred to Jr./High School I found out what a blessing rain was to my life. When it rained, we went to school. When the weather was nice, during cotton season, we knew that we would be out of school on many days because we had to help with the crop. We would hide between rows in the field when the school bus came along because we didn't want the other kids to know that we had to stay at home and pick cotton.

I don't remember many particulars about my junior and high school years. I do remember that schoolwork was not hard for me. My favorite subjects were shorthand, typing, and art. I didn't care for science, math, or history. I didn't have much confidence in myself and didn't seem to fit in anywhere. I was not allowed to attend many functions or to date. Whenever I asked to go to a game or some other function, my grandmother would always say, "I'm not raising any more babies". So, I got to a place where I stopped asking and just stayed at home. My grandmother meant well and perhaps if she had allowed me to go, I might have messed up.

It didn't kill me to stay at home all of the time but I can't relive those days. They are gone forever. Sometimes we underestimate what blessings are or are not.

The house and yard work continued to be the main part of my life after school and I remember spending a lot of time perfecting the chores that I was assigned to do. We didn't have as much play time as the other kids – there were just too many chores to be done before night came. My brother who was a year older than I was did not help with the chores very much. He would go and play and I would be left to do the chores. I used to get spankings when I disobeyed. The belt used was of thick leather. No matter where we hid that belt, when my grandmother was ready to tan our hides, she would find it. My brother did not get many spankings. He would get a "Boy, I don't know what I'm going to do with you" and that would be the end of it for him. He was my grandmother's favorite child. I remember the times she would slip him money for school. She would make me do things for him and she would not make him do things for me.

As I said earlier, there were no inside plumbing at our house. We had an **outside** pump and we had an **outside** toilet. We had no bathrooms or telephones until 1969. We bathed in a large tub that we had to fill with water heated on the stove.

One funny recollection of my growing up was a misunderstanding that my brother and I had. We thought that my grandmother was hiding chocolate candy from us in the middle drawer of her dresser. We had seen her go in the drawer and take pieces of the chocolate candy. Only it wasn't candy; it was a laxative called ex-lax. Needless to say, she left to go to church one Sunday evening and we decided we were going to get a few pieces of that candy. Surely, she wouldn't miss it.

We just couldn't understand why she wouldn't allow us to have any because she shared everything with us. When she returned, she did not have to ask us what happened – we were spending a lot of time running to the outside toilet.

My grandfather was an alcoholic and he physically attacked my grandmother on many occasions while accusing her of things she simply was not guilty of doing. I don't know how she put up with him for so many years. In his drunkenness, he would almost always go for his rifle, shotgun, or pistol when he returned home from his many drinking sprees. He would constantly curse us out (waking up everyone in the house) and then begin shooting at us. We would be running through the woods like rabbits. We usually ended up at his mom's house in the woods behind our house. He would follow us leaving the gun behind a tree as though he had done nothing. It was only the Lord that kept us alive.

One night when he came home drunk and after my grandmother had helped him into bed, he called for her. When she went back to the bedroom, he was lying there with his pistol in hand. The pistol was loaded with bullets, the safety latch was off, and he told her that he was going to kill her. I stepped in between the pistol and my grandmother, and I told him that he would have to kill me first. He pulled the trigger but NOTHING happened. I managed to wrestle it out of his hands. I know that God was with us.

My mother's parents raised my brother C, and me. When my brother and I were young, my mother ran away from home because my grandparents were so strict on her. When I graduated from high school, my grandparents were older and could use help so I decided to stay around to help them. I ended up leaving as my mother had because they were too strict with me. I almost had a nervous breakdown because I catered to their every wish, feeling guilty if I disagreed in any way with what they said or did. Even though I had graduated from high school and had a job, they could only see me as a teenager who needed them to make all my decisions.

For most of our lives, my grandparents led us to believe that our mom just ran off and didn't want us, but it wasn't that way at all. When my mom left, she went to North Carolina where she met and married a wonderful man (Allen V. Pierce) who was truly sent by God. She had 3 more children. When she got situated and came back for us, my grandparents would not allow her to take us.

She knew that legally she could get us but for fear of bringing about more of a strain on their relationship and the fact that she knew we were being cared for, she allowed us to stay with them. They never allowed my brother and I to go and visit our mother without them. I don't know if they were afraid that we'd learn the truth about everything or if they afraid we would not have enough love to go around.

My mother would visit us but the truths about her life at home were not discussed until I became an adult and after the passing away of my grandparents. My mother and I talked extensively after that. We became close...our relationship was more like "sister to sister" rather than "mother to daughter". I enjoyed the times we spent together and I looked forward to us spending more time together. That dream died when I went to Saudi Arabia. I was in the last week of my 6-month tour when my mom had a stroke and died 2 weeks after my return to the country. That was one of the biggest hurdles for me to overcome in my life. I am convinced that by <u>seeing her faith in God in action</u>, and <u>my faith in God</u> took me over that hurdle.

I met my father, Frazier, after I became an adult. When I was about 8 or 9 years old, he came to see me at my grandparents' house. I didn't realize who he was but I felt very close to him. Later in my life, my mother told me that he did not accept me as his child when she told him that she was pregnant. He joined the U.S. Army and later was united in marriage to another woman. When I was older, I met his sisters and one of them (Aunt Martha) told me that he lived in Philadelphia. She gave me his telephone number and arranged for us to come together and it was a wonderful meeting. We kept in touch and I had looked forward to spending more time with him. That dream died also, because after only three visits and a few phone calls, he passed away.

I miss my Mother and my Father and wish that I could have gotten to know them better. Aunt Martha (my father's sister) was one that the Lord had sent to me. She told me stories about the family and introduced me to his side of my family. She always worked to bring and keep the family together. I admired her for her great faith in God also. She passed away in 2001. I miss her so much.

My great grandfather Charlie was one of the sweetest men I've ever met. He was calm, loving, and had a reassuring spirit. I can see him now. He used to walk with his hands behind his back.

He always took great grandmother to church, but I never once saw him inside of the church as we grew up. My great grandmother was always in there but he, dressed in his suit and looking good, would always sit on the back steps of the church. I never asked him why he didn't go inside or if he could hear the sermons being preached on the outside. All I know is that his spirit was more attuned to God than many of those who frequented the inside of the church all the time. My great grandmother was also a blessing. She was like one of the old oak trees that grew where we lived. She was strong and stood many tests of time. She outlived most of her relatives, and was in her right mind until my mother passed away. Something changed in her mind at that time.

A wonderful remembrance of the days and times when I was younger was the respect that younger people had for adults, especially elderly folks. A shortcoming for that time was the fact that the parents didn't share a lot with the younger people. They would hide issues about diseases or sicknesses and they didn't share much about sex. Racism was and continue to be an issue. I remember the separate water fountains, bath rooms, doctor offices, restaurants, etc.

As I now have an understanding of people being called and walking in the place God has for them, there was one man I am convinced that he was definitely in his place...our principal in high school. After my grandmother, Mr. Charles E. Murray was my first role model. He did everything with excellency and I appreciate that example to this day. One of his favorite sayings was: *People do according to their understanding*.

I graduated from high school in 1970 and worked at a sewing factory for a year. That was not the answer for the rest of my life. I went to New York to my sister and later joined Job Corps in Jersey City, New Jersey. I had my first encounter with the gay community - lesbians...quite an eye opener. Completed my course and graduated after 10 months of training. I worked for the U.S. Department of Labor – OSHA for two years after that and decided to join the U.S. Air Force in May of 1975.

THINGS I LEARNED IN THE EARLIER YEARS OF MY LIFE:

I learned that the enemy comes early to hinder the plans of God but he cannot stop what the Creator has ordained.

I learned that the time and place where I grew up was orchestrated by God. We can't choose where we come from but we can choose where we are going. We can choose to continue to grow up and to learn from life or we can choose to take life's tests over and over and over again.

I learned to appreciate honesty, hard work, discipline, respect, and to appreciate technology and advancement. Discipline is something I'm still working on to this day.

I learned that being a member of a church does not make you a Christian.
I understand that having been made to attend Church (including Sunday School) provided a foundation for me. At church, I learned about Christ, but later I came to know Christ personally.

I learned that we don't always see things in the same light and that things are not always what they seem.

I learned forgiveness when I ignorantly hated my grandfather for being an alcoholic. Being ignorant as to what the real problem was (a spirit that had him bound) and ignorant of the way in which to deal with the problem. I came to the truth of the matter and forgave him. We wrestle not against flesh and blood….

I also learned that Romans 8:28 is true; that all things work together for good to them that love the Lord and are the called according to His purpose. My grandfather being an alcoholic deterred me from alcohol/drug abuse.

I learned that having favorites between or among siblings is not good, nor is it right.

Victoria R. Bradley

I learned that our attitudes determine our altitudes. My grandmother helped me out with that every time she tanned my backside. She broke that stubborn, rebellious spirit that would otherwise influence my life. Those spankings did not kill me – they reinforced her love.

I learned that the spirit of racism was prevalent in our community but my grandmother taught us to love everybody, and I'm grateful for that. There is nothing more powerful.

I learned this about needing eyeglasses. Isn't it funny how we think we're seeing clearly but we truly are not seeing clearly at all. Many times we need clarity and don't even know it.

I learned that life is all about choices. It's all about sowing and reaping. And that the most important things are love – and obedience.

I learned that the absence of a good father figure at home makes it harder to see the love of our heavenly father. **Fathers, be <u>fathers</u> to your children!!!**

THINGS I LEARNED ABOUT RELATIONSHIP BETWEEN SISTERS AND BROTHERS:

I learned that love does not require a response. Even though we expect and desire siblings' responses to be mutual, that's not always the case. I love my sisters and brothers in spite of because Jesus loves me in spite of me. His love is unconditional so mine is too.

I also learned that my biological siblings are not my only family. The entire body of Christ is my family. So, I am blessed, no matter where I go, because I have family everywhere.

The enemy will use those closest to you to invoke discouragement and to get you off focus because they don't respond the way you may wish them to, but that's only a gnat. Love keeps you focused and encouraged.

I learned that all relationships are important no matter who they involve (sisters and brothers by blood or by spirit, and your fellowman).

I also learned that our journeys involve people that walk with us *some of the way*, others that travel with us *all of the way*, and those that are *not to walk with us at all*. If they add to you, well; if they take away from you, separate from them.

I once felt that staying in touch with them was so important, but the Lord even tells us not to put our trust in any man, and that even if our mothers and fathers forsake us, He will take us up.

Victoria R. Bradley

THINGS I LEARNED THROUGHOUT MY MILITARY CAREER:

I had much to learn as I embarked on this assignment. I learned that racism is everywhere (subtle or obvious). I learned to love my enemy and to do good to them that spitefully used me.

I learned that whatever it is that God has ordained for your life will be just that if we agree with Him.

I learned that spirits are real and they are transferable.

I learned the difference between fact and truth. I came to understand that situations, conditions, and circumstances are all temporary but the truth always prevails and is eternal.

I came to understand that salvation included everything (not just eternal life), but abundant life here and now. God wants us whole, not just partly whole.

I learned that we can grow in the Lord or we can remain babies in Christ.

I learned that the Lord has my back all the time and I saw His hands upon my life so many times and in so many ways. Just because He chooses to hide himself from us at certain times does not mean He is not with us. And, just because we can't see how He is working things out for us doesn't mean that He isn't working. I really learned to trust Him.

I learned to recognize the enemy and his tactics because I continued to grow in God.

I learned that we need the negatives to balance out the positives in our lives. If we had no negatives, we would not appreciate the positives. Everything will not be to our liking but as we obey the commands of the ones having rule over us at the time, we'll see that the seasons will change.

I learned that life may throw curves at you at times when you're trying to steer clearly ahead but we must learn to make adjustments and move on. I learned to move pass rejection and hatred coming from others.

I learned discipline, learned to walk alone, learned to use each situation as a stepping stone to where I was going.

I learned that racism is everywhere but God is too.

THINGS I LEARNED ABOUT MARRIAGE:

I learned that Love (agape) is the basic foundation that is needed for each individual before engaging in a relationship. When we don't truly understand what Love is, we can't love each other.

I learned that we need to seek God about a mate and wait for that mate.

I learned that taking time to get to know one another is definitely necessary.

I learned that each individual needs to be broken, and yet be whole before you can be an effective mate. Otherwise, you may be in a contract and not a covenant.

I learned that communication is so very important and that becoming friends first is a must.

I learned that we need to look at what's inside of a person, and not just focus on what's on the outside.

I learned that hanging in there and working at the relationship once you're married is a plus. It does pay off, even though it may not always change the relationship. Everything requires work if it's worth anything.

I learned that you can be in church per say and not in Christ. That being said, you can still be unequally yoked to someone in the church.

I learned that we need to know who we are, and whose we are, before we enter into any kind of relationship.

I understand that marriage is God's order for the family and I don't take it lightly.

I understand that it is best to be friends first, then you can relate (relationship). And before that, God has to be first before we can understand what "Love" is, for He is love. Love is not lust, and is not based on outward appearance or circumstances. There must be trust and communication.

I learned that you need to be a whole person before getting involved with another person, and you need to make sure the other person is whole. A half person involved with another half person does not make a whole. Maturity is very important.

I now understand that we need to cover our mates – in love, in prayer, in faith, in situations, circumstances, and conditions.

I learned that a giver and a taker can never be in agreement.

I learned that selfishness has no place in a marriage.

I learned that divorce is not God's divine order.

Victoria R. Bradley

THINGS I LEARNED FROM BEING ON FOREIGN SOIL:

I learned that attacks come mainly through people who are supposed to be closest to you – family, friends, sisters and brothers in Christ, etc., but I also learned that we wrestle not against flesh and blood but spirits.

I learned that the Holy Spirit is always present to help if you belong to the Master.

I learned that death is not the end for us but the beginning. That we are not here to stay but are just passing through this earth. We are lent to each other for a season – no one said that we would be here (on this earth) for each other forever.

I learned that the enemy of God tempts and condemns, but God, our Father tests and convicts.

I learned that life here is a temporary assignment with many tests, trials, temptations.

I learned that adversity, difficulty, and rejection are all a part of the maturing process and that they do also work together for our good and God's purpose.

I learned to appreciate our country and heritage. No matter how messed up America is, there is no place like home. I also learned how to respect other nationalities and their heritage.

So many attacks have come my way. The Word of God tells me that many are the afflictions of the righteous but God delivers us from them all.

I learned that the Word of God is true no matter what. Whether we believe it or not, it remains to be true.

I saw that my child's faith pleased God. He was an example to us of the kind of faith we are to have as adults. If we are His, we are to be humble like little children.

I learned that we won't always understand but we are to trust God regardless. His thoughts and His ways are so much higher and so far above ours and we are not God – we're made in His image and likeness, given power and authority, but we are not Him.

I learned that authority is given to Priests and Kings to carry out what God has established. What we believe is so very important, because what we believe is what we act on.

I learned that there are different types of prayer and different levels of prayer. I became aware for the first time of the meaning of "standing in the gap" for another person.

I learned that many of our experiences can't be explained but they are all wrought in our lives for a reason and with a purpose.

I must continue to seek the Lord in all that there is. He is the only answer for us today.

THINGS I LEARNED ABOUT REARING CHILDREN:

I learned quickly what "tough love" was all about. I never dreamed that I would have to use tough love with my sons – we live and we learn.

I understand that my two sons have different personalities but I love them both the same. One is more aggressive and outspoken and the other son is more passive, and quiet. I learned how to deal with them in different ways but exemplifying the same love.

I learned to separate the child from the spirit. I had to address the spirit and yet deal with the child. I learned to let go of anger at my child and attack the source, which was the spirit behind him. Then, I embraced the Master.

I learned how to plead the blood of Jesus over my children.

I learned to agree with and confess what the Lord said concerning my children:
- that He's promised to bless the fruit of my womb
- that they will go on to know the Lord
- that we are to train them up in the way they should go….
- that me and my children would be blessed as we are spiritual seeds of Abraham

I saw how the enemy uses our children or anyone else who will allow him to use them to come against us. I've learned to squash him with the Word of God. I refused to have bad nerves, a bad heart, high blood pressure, insanity, or an early death from stress because of family members or family enemies.

I learned to pray and seek the Lord even the more and to continue trusting Him with my children. We are all his children and my children were His first before they were mine. So, He has lent them to me and I have lent them back to Him.

I learned how to war against the enemy that comes after my seed. He cannot have what the Lord has given me and I know that he cannot have what I've given to the Lord.

I learned that tests and trials come to make us strong. Our faith **must be** tested. I also learned that suffering is a part of living as we die to self.

I learned that we bring many things upon ourselves because of our disobedience and not listening to the Lord.

I learned that the enemy sends temptations and that he works for the Lord. He can do no more than what God allows. The Lord works all things out for our good and His purpose if we love Him and are called according to His purpose. The thief (in whatever form) comes to steal, kill and destroy but Jesus came that we might have life and that more abundantly.

I've learned to trust in the Lord with all my heart (not in man) and not to lean to my own understanding.

I learned that all sickness is not unto death just as the Bible says.

I learned that I have a high tolerance for pain.

I learned that death cannot touch you when the Lord has not given it permission to.

I learned that the Lord has people in places for you that you know nothing about. That's why we are to trust in Him with all of our hearts and lean not to our own understanding---especially when we can't see the way.

Victoria R. Bradley

MASTER'S DEGREE

SYLLABUS FOR THE "MASTER'S DEGREE OF LIFE" COURSE

A MESSAGE FROM THE DEAN – GOD Himself

> OUR Creator, Maker, Savior, Lord, Alpha and Omega, Redeemer, Righteousness, Righteous Judge, Salvation, Source, Foundation, Structure, Song, Rock, Strength, Refuge, Shield, Buckler, Banner, Balance, Fortress, High Tower, I am that I am, Light, Keeper, Protector, Provider, Healer, King of Kings, Lord of Lords, Counselor, Joy, Peace, Victory, Sustainer, Love, Lover, Everything!

Yes, I am your Creator, and maker, the <u>Master</u> of the Universe. I knew you before you were born and I made you in my likeness and image.

You can trust me. I've made you many promises and I am not slack concerning my promises.

During this life course, you will either accept me (pass) and graduate or you will reject me (fail) and be left behind.

I will be your Savior, and your Lord if you allow me to be. I can be your Everything, but the choice is yours. I encourage you to choose this day whom you will serve.

In this earthly class, there is only One Vision: Mine.

Foundationally Accredited by the Highest Learning Source and Based on Two Commandments:

1. Love God with All Your Heart
2. Love Your Neighbor as Yourself

Victoria R. Bradley

SCHOOL OF EXCELLENCE	<u>L</u> <u>I</u> <u>F</u> <u>E</u> ON EARTH
ADMISSION CRITERIA	YOUR BIRTH
ADMISSION PROCEDURES	GROWTH (Infant, Child, Adult)
ADMISSION APPLICATION	Apply in Person (Only One Way)
RE-ADMISSION/RE-ENTRY	Repentance
CONTINUING STUDENTS	Forgiven
NONDISCRIMINATION	Anyone, Everyone
CLASSROOM OR ONLINE	One Teacher (The Holy Spirit)
WITHDRAWALS	YOUR DEATH
PROBATION OR WARNING	The Gift of God is Eternal Life / The Wages of Sin is Death
COURSE EXEMPTION	Only Those Who Have Not Been
STUDENT CONDUCT	Your Conduct Must Be Holy
MAJORS, MINORS, & CONCENTRATIONS	Major in God, Minor in Satan, and Self, and Stay Focused
ELECTIVES	You May Elect to Excel by your Obedience for Extra Rewards
PRIVACY OF RECORDS	Everything about you is kept In confidence in HIM

LENGTH OF COURSE……………………………………...LIFETIME – ETERNITY

During this course, you must Appeal to your Senses (Spiritual more than Natural):

- *Engage listening skills –* **Ear**
- *Be very observant –* **Eyes**
- *Stay focused –* **Heart**
- *Oral Participation –* **Mouth**
- *Stay Connected –* **Body**

CLASS TIME (CHRONOS/SPIRIT)……………………….Past, Present, Future
                                                                Daily, 24/7, *All Seasons

*Note: The Seasons always Change.

LOCATION………………………………………………………….Anywhere/Everywhere

PREREQUISITE:
- Believe in the Bible and it's Author
- Genesis 1:1 …In the beginning God…
- Hebrews 11:6 …must believe that He is who He says He is…
 …agree with all that He says

REQUISITE:

Act on what you believe – Accept the free gift of salvation
- John 3:16 God so Loved the World, that He Gave…
- Romans 10:9-10 Believe in your heart, confess with your
- Romans 10:13 mouth…./Whosoever call on the Name…
- 2 Corinthians 4:13 I believed, and therefore have I spoken

REGISTRATION:
- SALVATION – Abundant Life (now) and Eternal Life (now and forever)
- John 10:10 I am come that they might have life, and that they might have it more abundantly.

TEACHER: The Holy Spirit
- John 14:16, 26 (Comforter, Spirit of truth, Holy Ghost)

TUITION………….Free   (Costs only 'yourself' according to Luke 14:26-33)

Your "<u>self</u>" must be hated (by you), must be crucified (by you), must be humbled (by you), must be tested (by Him), must be chastened (by Him).

BOOKS REQUIRED……………………..The Bible, Concordance, Dictionary, Notebooks, Other Testimonial Material (As directed by the Holy Spirit)

SPIRITUAL SUPPLIES NEEDED:

    Compass   -   sets the course
    Protractor -   makes right angles
    Pen   -   for the ready writer
    Notebook   -   keep notes daily

CURRICULUM:

Daily Presence	You must be present and accounted for every day. (In Him you live, move, and be)
Class Participation	If you are truly present and accounted for, then, you must participate in class. (We are workers together with Him)
Special Projects	From time to time, the teacher will assign you to special projects, sometimes INDIVIDUALLY, sometimes COLLECTIVELY, and sometimes CORPORATELY. Be prepared.
Homework	No time to slack off. Homework assignments are necessary. Everything can't be done in one place. Make sure home is in order first.
Hands-On Training	You will get to apply the knowledge you've attained. You will have to put into practice the things you have learned. You can't just be a hearer, but you must be a doer also.
Study & Review 1 Thessalonian 4:11 2 Timothy 2:15	Study, read, review, meditate. Study to be approved; eat, grow. You can't pray what you don't know.
Stay Synchronized	Spirit, Soul, Body

TESTING

Tests are given throughout the course. You will have pop quizzes, scheduled, and unscheduled tests (multiple-choice, questions, and essays). Bonus Points called "Favor" will apply to many of the tests. Other factors are considered before your final grade is computed.

Pre-Test Exam (Beginning)

The first part of your life course is called the Pre-Test. This is the time before you know <u>Who you are</u> and <u>Who He is</u>…You are literally <u>feeling</u> your way – No faith established yet. You can't fail this test. You are still a babe on milk, no strong meats, BUT YOU ARE GOING TO THE OTHER SIDE.

Mid Term Exam (Midway)

In the middle of your journey, you will encounter turbulence. No one told you, uh? It's okay. Everyone experiences some storms. You can't appreciate them until you've come through them. Your diet is changing now from milk to more solid stuff. Don't forget the simplicity of the foundational meal of milk. Just know that you will survive, BECAUSE YOU ARE GOING TO THE OTHER SIDE.

Final Exam (End)

Latter part of your journey, you will have many testimonies by this time, and your diet will have changed. You're on strong meat and drink – Angus Steak and Potatoes, plus Dessert. Now you just continue to apply all that you have learned, continue to learn, and walk in all the truth that you know. Just steady the course and you will arrive safely, suddenly, ON THE OTHER SIDE.

GRADES

- A for Excellence
- B for Better
- C for Careful
- D for Doubtful
- F for Failure
- I for Incomplete

Field Trips
- Home Missions
- Local Missions

- National Missions
- International Missions

Your Mission Field begins outside of You. You are a Missionary at home, at church, in school, at work, in your neighborhood, in the market place. Your Missionary work may always be local in the natural. For some, their Mission extends outside of their physical boundaries of City and State or Country to Other Countries. Your Mission Abroad may only be in Intercessory Prayer or Financial Support. Wherever and Whatever the Master has ordained, let it be.

Matthew 28:19-20   Luke 14:23

CLASSES

Title:	**Your Relationship with:**
Self 100	God
Self 101	Spouse
Self 102	Children
Self 103	Neighbors
Self 104	Blood Family
Self 105	Church Family
Self 106	Extended Family
Self 107	The World

Classes subject to change by the Holy Spirit. In fact, **Everything** is subject to change by the Holy Spirit!

BASIC FOUNDATION

Word Meaning

Love...(God is love); To hold dear; to take pleasure in; strong affection; unconditional; suffers long; is kind; envies not; is not rash or puffed up; does not behave itself unseemly; is unselfish; not easily provoked; forgives; thinks no evil; does not rejoice in iniquity but rejoices in truth; bears all things; believes all things; hopes all things, endures all things; never fails. Love covers a multitude of sin; is greater than faith (because faith works by love) and hope; Perfect love casts out fear.

Faith...(Now faith) is the substance and the evidence of things hoped for and not yet seen; works by love; our faith makes us whole; without it we can't please God. Faith is simply knowing God!

Hope...a desire with expectation of fulfillment; reliance; trust; to long for with expectation of obtainment; does not make ashamed; lively.

Belief/Believe...conviction of the truth of the word of God or the reality of something; faith; credit; acceptance; intellectual assent; to have a firm conviction as to the reality or goodness of something; to accept trustfully and on faith; think; to hold an opinion; consider to be true or honest.

Trust...assured reliance on the character, ability, strength or truth of someone or something; confidence placed; dependence on; hope; reliance without fear or misgiving; to rely on the accuracy of.

Truth...true; fidelity; constancy; sincerity in action, character and utterance; that body of real things, events and facts; the body of true statements and propositions.

Obedience...act of obeying; submissive to the command of authority; willing to obey; compliance with the demands or requests of one in authority; to submit readily to the guidance or control of; having a character that permits easy handling or managing; a willingness to yield or to cooperate; to conform to or comply with.

Destiny...a predetermined course of events often held to be an irresistible power; an appointment; to decree beforehand; designate; assign; dedicate in advance; set apart for a specific purpose.

Victory...fulfilled; winning or conquest; achievement of mastery or success in a struggle or endeavor against odds or difficulties; the overcoming of an enemy or antagonist.

Salvation...a free gift; received by faith; deliverance from the power and effects of sin; liberation from ignorance or illusion; preservation from destruction or failure; deliverance from danger.

Peace...a state of tranquility or quiet; a state of security or order; freedom from oppressive thoughts or emotions; harmony.

Authority...Power to influence or command thought, opinion, or behavior; government.

Passion...The sufferings of Christ between the night of the Last Supper and His death; emotion distinguished from reason; intense; driving; overmastering feeling or conviction; ardent affection; love; a strong desire for or devotion to; fervor, enthusiasm, zeal.

Holy Spirit...The Spirit of God given to us by God to assist us throughout the entire course.

Fruit of the Spirit...Love, joy, peace, longsuffering, gentleness, goodness, faith, meekness, temperance.

Works of the Flesh...Adultery (immorality), fornication (impurity), uncleanness (indecency), lasciviousness, idolatry, witchcraft (sorcery), hatred (anger/strife/enmity), jealousy (envying), selfishness, murders, divisions (dissensions), drunkenness (reveling/carousing).

Victoria R. Bradley

What You Need to **_Know_** to Successfully Pass This Course

YOU NEED TO KNOW:

1. Who God Is
2. Who You Are and Whose You Are
3. That God is Love
4. That God is Who He says He Is
5. That God is No Respect of Persons
6. That God Cannot Lie
7. That God is Faithful
8. That God's Word does not Return unto Him Void
9. That God did not Give You the Spirit of Fear
10. That God is a Jealous God
11. That God will Never Fail You, Nor Forsake You
12. That You have a Destiny
13. That this is Not Your Home
14. That the Battle is not Yours, but the Lord's
15. That the Victory is Already Yours
16. That You are Chosen by God
17. That You are Fearfully and Wonderfully Made
18. That You are Male or Female
19. That You've been given Everything pertaining to Life & Godliness
20. That You Reap What You Sow
21. That You are to Reflect the Sun (Son)
22. That Obedience is Better than Sacrifice
23. That there is Power in Agreement
24. That You are Being Processed by God
25. That Christ is being Formed in You
26. That Success does not Depend on What You Have or Have Not
27. That All things are Working Together for Your Good
28. That Man does not Live by Bread Alone, but By The Word of God
29. That No Flesh should Glory in His Presence
30. That Your Faith should Not Stand in the Wisdom of Men, but in the Power of God
31. That You have the Mind of Christ and the Wisdom of God
32. That You are the Temple of God and The Spirit of God Dwells in You

33. That Life and Death is in the Power of the Tongue
34. That Fear is the Beginning of Wisdom
35. That God is Faithful and He will not allow you to be Tempted Above that You are able to bear

WE NEED WISE COUNSEL – KNOWLEDGE, WISDOM, UNDERSTANDING

> **A wise man will hear, and will increase learning; and a man of understanding shall attain unto wise counsels.**
> **Proverbs 1:5**
>
> **The fear of the Lord is the beginning of knowledge...**
> **Proverbs 1:7**
>
> **...incline thine ear unto wisdom, and apply thine heart to understanding;...**
> **Proverbs 2:2**
>
> **For the Lord giveth wisdom: out of his mouth cometh knowledge and understanding.**
> **Proverbs 2:6**

What You Need to *Be* Throughout This Course

YOU NEED TO BE:

1. Be (Present and Active)
2. Believe
3. Be Holy for He is Holy
4. Be Perfect for He is Perfect
5. Be Faithful
6. Be Encouraged
7. Be Thankful
8. Be Obedient
9. Be Wise
10. Be Sincere
11. Be Transparent
12. Be Merciful
13. Be Steadfast and unmovable
14. Be Strong
15. Be Still and Know that He is God
16. Be of a Good Courage
17. Be a True Worshipper
18. Be a Tither
19. Be Fully Persuaded
20. Be Blessed
21. Be Fruitful and Multiply
22. Be Led by the Spirit
23. Be Kind One to Another
24. Be Anxious for Nothing
25. Be a Follower of God
26. Be a Cheerful Giver
27. Be Slow to Speak, but Swift to Hear
28. Be a Good Steward
29. Be Free because the Son has made You Free
30. Be a Doer of the Word and Not a Hearer Only
31. Be it Unto You as He has Said
32. Be not High-Minded, but Fear

Be One of the <u>Patriarchs</u> of Faith

<u>Be a "Abram"</u>……

By faith, when God called him to leave his comfort zone, he obeyed, not knowing exactly where he was going. (Gen 15:6/Heb 11:8)

He believed in the Lord and was counted as righteous. Abraham hoped against hope, and being not weak in faith, he considered not the natural look of things; He staggered not at the promise of God through unbelief; but was strong in faith, giving glory to God; and being fully persuaded that what He had promised, He was able also to perform. (Rom 4:16-22)

<u>Be a "Noah"</u>………

He walked with God and did according to all that the Lord commanded. By faith, he being warned of God of things not seen as yet, moved with fear, prepared an ark to the saving of his house. (Gen 6:9/7:5; Heb 11:7)

<u>Be a "Enoch"</u>……

He walked with God and he was not for God took him. The record he left was that he pleased God.
(Gen 5:24)

<u>Be a "Joshua"</u>…….

He left nothing undone of all that the Lord commanded Moses. God commanded him to be strong and of a good courage. He obeyed God and the walls of Jericho came down…."as for me and my house, we will serve the Lord." (Josh 1:6-7/6:20/11:15/24:15)

<u>Be a "Caleb"</u>………

He had another spirit (not doubtful) and wholly followed the Lord; Caleb and Joshua were the only ones that came up out of Egypt 20 years and older to enter the Promised Land. (Num 13:30/14:8-9,30/32:12)

Victoria R. Bradley

<u>Be a "David"</u>…….

David was taken from the sheepfolds and was brought to feed Jacob his people and Israel his inheritance. He fed them according to the integrity of his heart; and guided them by the skillfulness of his hands

What You Need to **_Do_** In This Course

(Your Doing Comes Out of Your Being)

YOU NEED TO:

1. Seek First the Kingdom of God and His Righteousness
2. Walk in Love
3. Walk by Faith
4. Forget the Past
5. Forgive All
6. Trust in the Lord with All Your Heart
7. Acknowledge the Lord in All Your Ways; He Will Direct Your Path
8. In Everything, Give Thanks
9. Work Out Your Own Soul Salvation
10. Work While It's Day for the Night Cometh When No Man Can Work
11. Pray without Ceasing
12. Watch and Pray
13. Praise God from Whom All Blessings Flow
14. Dominate, Subdue, Rule, and Reign
15. Study to Show Yourself Approved
16. Study to Be Quiet
17. Do unto Others as You would have them Do unto You
18. Give and It shall be Given unto You
19. Serve the Lord with Gladness
20. Rejoice
21. Count it all Joy when You Fall into Divers Temptations
22. Fellowship with Other Believers

What You **_Should Not Do_** In This Course

1. Don't Look Back; You Will Trip Up
2. Don't Despise Your Birthright; It Belongs to You
3. Don't Murmur or Complain; Accept What God Allows
4. Despise not small beginnings; They turn into large endings
5. Do not Add to or Take Away ought from the Word of the Lord

Victoria R. Bradley

What To _**Think**_ As You Go Along The Way

1. Think on these things – whatsoever things are true, honest, just, pure, lovely, and of a good report.   (Phil 4:8)

2. Think big for as a man thinks in his heart, so is he.   (Prov 23:7)

3. Wherefore let him that Thinks he stand take heed lest he fall.

4. Think it not Strange concerning the fiery trial which is to try you as though some strange thing happened unto you; but rejoice, inasmuch as you are partakers of Christ's suffering……
(1 Pet 4:12)

5. Think soberly – do not think of yourself more highly than you ought to think….   (Rom 12:3)

GUESS WHAT THE MASTER THINKS OF YOU:

In Jeremiah 29:11 He Says…

> **For I know the thoughts that I think toward you, says the Lord, thoughts of peace, and not of evil, to give you an expected end.**

OUR WEAPONS OF WARFARE

There is a bully at school who comes seeking whom he may devour; always trying to take what does not belong to him. He comes to steal, kill, and destroy. We must fight him with the weapons that our Master has provided for us. Oh, it will be a good fight (of faith) because we win!

The Word of God
Jesus (His Name and His Blood)
Holy Spirit
Angels
Our Voice
Our Anointing
Prayer
Praise
Worship
Faith
Love
Joy
Peace
Favor
Obedience
Knowledge
Wisdom
Understanding
Forgiveness
Truth
Boldness
Promises of God
Place of Rest
Fear of God
Sincerity
Dominion
Tenacity
Discernment
Divine Order

Victoria R. Bradley

Questions to Ask Yourself During This Course

Is anything too hard for the Lord?
Gen 18:14

Is the Lord's hand waxed short?
Num 11:23

Have I now any power at all to say anything? God is not a man, that He should lie, neither the son of man that He should repent; has He said and shall He not do it? Or has He spoken, and shall He not make it good?
Num 22:38/23:19

For what nation is there so great, who has God so nigh unto them, as the Lord Our God is in all things that we call upon him for?
Deut 4:7

Is not the Lord your father that has brought you? Has He not made you, and established you?
Deut 32:6, 18

How long are you slack to go to possess the land, which the Lord God of your fathers have given you?
Josh 18:3

What? Know you not that your body is the temple of the Holy Ghost which is in you, which you have of God, and you are not your own?
1 Cor 6:15

For who makes you to differ from another? And what do you have that you did not receive? Now if you did receive it, why do you glory as if you had not received it?
1 Cor 4:7

Know you not that they which run in a race run all, but one receives the prize? So run, that you may obtain. 1 Cor 9:24

Hindrances to Graduation

The <u>WAGES</u> of <u>SIN</u> is <u>DEATH</u>

Unforgiveness	Judging Others
False Witnessing	Lying
Blasphemy	Strife
Covetous	Murder
Malice	Drunkenness
Wickedness	Passiveness
Grudging	Stealing
Extortion	
Deception	
Devil Worship	
Jealousy	
Envy	
Gossiping	
Backbiting	
Sowing Discord	
Murmuring	
Complaining	
Hatred	
Anger	
Bitterness	
Selfishness	
Greed	
Love of Money	
Idolatry	
Adultery	
Fornication	
Abuse	
Lust	
Unbelief	
Doubting	
Uncleanness	
Rebellion	
Stubbornness	

Victoria R. Bradley

PRAYER FOR THE CLASSROOM

Father, in the name of Jesus, as we enter the doors of the classroom daily, may we endeavor to do all that you have ordained for us to do. Each day we ask that you would create in each of us a clean heart and renew a right spirit within us.

Father, we humbly submit our entire selves (spirit, soul, and body) to you. Do what you want to do for we belong to you. Bring glory to yourself.

Feed us until we want no more as we worship you in spirit and in truth. We realize that we are here to SERVE and to GLORIFY you so that you may be REVEALED in us.

You have not left us alone. You have given us your Spirit. Help us Lord, to respect and obey our Teacher. You have sent him to us to instruct, direct, and teach us; to bring to our remembrance what you spoke to us before we took on flesh; to keep us and to help us in those subjects where we're weak. We invite Him to reign in our lives. We thank you also for your angels that you have given charge over us to keep us in all our ways.

We awake each day with joyous anticipation and expectation for your manifested glory in our lives. Thank you for your new mercies every morning.

                                              In Jesus' Name,

                                              AMEN

Teach Me Your Way, Oh Lord

_____
(Student's Name)

CONGRATULATIONS, YOU MADE IT!

Well Done, Good and Faithful Servant; Enter into the Joy of the Lord.
You fought a Good Fight – You kept the Faith.

Victoria R. Bradley

MASTER

"Re-"

LET'S DO IT AGAIN

Everything in God is NOW as we position ourselves in the right place. Our Father has given us everything pertaining to life and to godliness. From our natural beginning as we come through the flesh, we find ourselves in a fallen position. God, in His infinite wisdom, has provided a way for us to get up. We've got to get up or get back up.

If you've never repented or if you have repented but backslid, it's time to get up and get back on top. Refuse to stay on the bottom or even in-between. We are ordained and destined for the penthouse; not the basement.

The title of an old R&B song came to mind as I thought about us returning to our right position in God, "Let's do it again." "RE" is a prefix which means AGAIN, for a second time, anew, in a new or different form, back, backward; and that's where the name of this book came from. Open up your Bibles, let's see what our creator says about it.

Matthew 3:1-6 speaks to us about repenting, for the Kingdom of heaven is at hand.

John 3:1-8 speaks to us about being born again, for one cannot see the Kingdom of God without being born of water and the Spirit.

Acts 2:38 speaks to us about repentance and baptism for the remission of sins, and the promise of the gift of the Holy Spirit.

1 Peter 1:3-5, 18, 19, 23 speaks to us of being begotten again; not being redeemed with corruptible things or seed but with the incorruptible, precious blood of Jesus through the word of God...which lives and abides forever.

2 Peter 3:9 speaks to us about God's longsuffering towards us in order for us to come to repentance.

So, however we perceive it (born again, repentance, begotten again, redeemed, converted), let the main thing be the main thing….REPENT, for the Kingdom of God is at hand.

In the following pages are 48 verbs (48 actions) that would truly activate us into our rightful place. Using the mirror of each verb, check yourself.

VERBS THAT REQUIRE ACTION

Repent
Revive
Renew
Resurrect
Remember
Regenerate
Refine
Redeem
Reconcile
Remit
Receive
Rebound
Reborn
Rebuild
Reacquaint
Readjust
Request
Revere
Reapply
Reassess
Reawaken
Recalculate
Recheck
Reconnect

Recover
Reconsider
Recuperate
Rededicate
Redetermine
Redo
Reemerge
Reestablish
Reexamine
Refeed
Reflect
Reform
Regard
Reheat
Regain
Rehab
Readdress
Rebirth
React
Relocate
Recall
Reverse
Reset
Rejoice

Victoria R. Bradley

Going Up instead of Staying Down

1

REPENT:

To change one's mind, to turn around, to get back on top

2

REVIVE:

To live again, to return to consciousness or life, to become active or flourishing again, to restore from a depressed, inactive or unused state, to bring back

3

RENEW:

To make like new, to restore to freshness, vigor or perfection, to begin or do again, to renew by cleansing, repairing, rebuilding

4

RESURRECT:

To bring back formation, to raise from the dead, to rise or use again, to surge or bring into view

5

REMEMBER:

To bring back to mind what is lost or scattered, to think of again, to remind, to retain or record

6

REGENERATE:

To become formed again, to change radically and for the better, to restore to original strength, to be spiritually reborn

7

REFINE:

To reduce to a pure state, to become perfected in excellence and clarity

8

REDEEM:

To take or buy back, to free from what distresses or harms, or from captivity, to release from blame or debt, to free from consequences of sin, to change for the better, to rescue

9

RECONCILE:

To restore to friendship of harmony, to make consistent or congruous, to account for

10

REMIT:

To release from the guilt or penalty of, to give relief, to lay aside

11

RECEIVE:

To take or acquire, to come into possession of, to support, to welcome or greet

12

REBOUND:

To spring back, to gain possession of, an upward leap or movement, recovery, a reaction to setback, frustration, or crisis

13

REBORN:

To be born again, regenerated, revived

14

REBUILD:

To build again, to make extensive repairs to, to reconstruct, to restore to a previous state

15

REACQUAINT:

To cause to know personally, to know firsthand again, to make familiar

16

READJUST:

To bring again to a more satisfactory state, to bring to a true or more effective relative position, to achieve balance

17

REQUEST:

To make inquiry, search, or pursue; an act or instance of seeking

18

REVERE:

To show devoted deferential honor to, worthy of great honor, worship, adoration, to admire profoundly and respectfully

19

REAPPLY:

To employ diligently or with close attention, to put into operation or effect again

20

REASSESS:

To determine the importance or value of again

21

REAWAKEN:

To cease sleeping, to become aroused or active again, to become conscious or aware, to stir up

22

RECALCULATE:

To solve, to prove the meaning of, to judge to be true, reckon

23

RECHECK:

To arrest, a sudden pause or break in a progression, to reprimand, to limit or restrain, a standard for testing and evaluating, examine

24

RECONNECT:

To become joined again, to make or establish a successful rapport with, to place or establish in relationship, related by blood or marriage, coherence, continuity

25

RECOVER:

To get back by legal process, to bring back to normal position or condition, to rescue, to save from loss and restore to usefulness

26

RECONSIDER:

To consider again with a view to changing or reversing

27

RECUPERATE:

To get back, regain, recover health or strength, restore

28

REDEDICATE:

To devote to the worship of a divine being, to set aside for a particular purpose, zealous

29

REDETERMINE:

To fix conclusively or authoritatively, to settle or decide, to come to an end or become void, settling, and ending controversy

30

REDO:

To do over or again

31

REEMERGE:

To become manifest, to come out into view, to rise from an obscure or inferior condition

32

REESTABLISH:

To make firm or stable again, to introduce and cause to grow and multiply, to institute permanently, to put into a favorable position again

33

REEXAMINE:

To test the condition of, to inquire into carefully, to investigate again

34

REFEED:

To become nourished or satisfied again, to become channeled or directed again

35

REFLECT:

To bend back, to give back, to exhibit as an image, likeness, or outline — mirror, to make manifest or apparent, to think quietly and calmly

36

REFORM:

To take form again, to improve by change, removal of faults or abuses, enforcing or introducing a better method or course of action, amendment of what is defective, corrupt, or depraved

37

REGARD:

To pay attention to, to take into consideration, to esteem, to respect, to admire

38

REHEAT:

To become warm or hot again

39

REGAIN:

To increase again in amount, magnitude, or degree

40

REHAB:

To restore to a former capacity or state, a rehabilitated house, to bring to a condition of health or useful and constructive activity

41

READDRESS:

To deal with again, to reanalyze, reconceive, reconsider, reexamine, review, rethink, recalculate

42

REBIRTH:

To be born again, a new or second birth, regenerated, rejuvenated, renewed, revived, resurrected; a return or renewal of vigor, freshness, or productivity

43

REACT:

To exert a return or counter acting influence, to act in opposition to a force or influence, to move in a reverse direction

44

RELOCATE:

To locate again, to move to a new location

45

RECALL:

A summons to return, remembrance of things learned or experienced

46

REVERSE:

To turn upside down or completely about in position or direction; opposite to a previous or normal condition

47

RESET:

To Set Again

48

REJOICE:

Jubilant, gladden, to give joy to, to have great delight in, glory, triumphant, content, please, satisfy

THE BODY

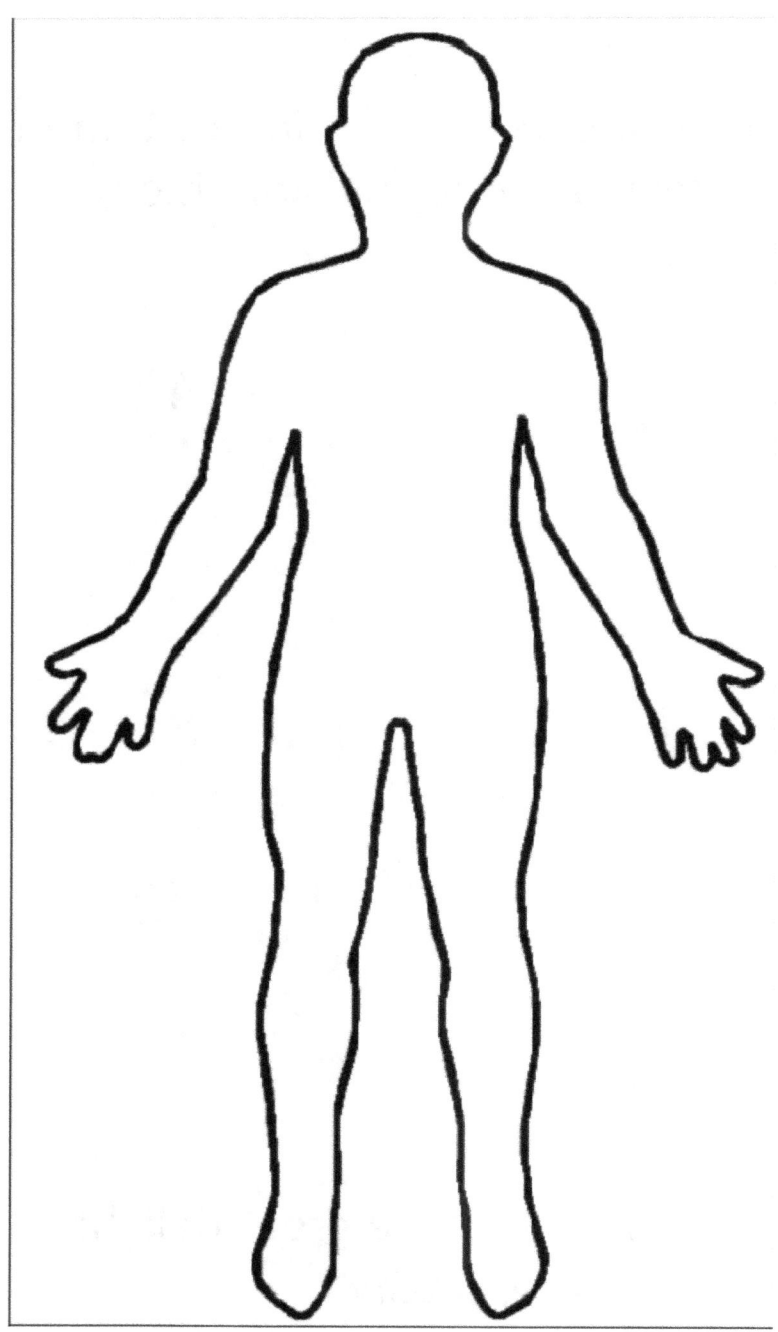

The Parts of the Body Addressed

THE HEAD (Mind, Brain, Soul)

THE EYES

THE NOSE

THE MOUTH (Voice/Teeth/Tongue)

THE EARS

THE NECK

THE HEART

THE SHOULDERS

THE ARMS

THE HANDS

THE WOMB

THE FEET

THE BONES

THE SKIN

THE INNER PARTS

THE SICK BODY

THE HEALTHY BODY

THE BODY OF CHRIST

INTRODUCTION

There are different types of bodies in the universe. "But God gives a body as He pleases, and to each seed its own body." There are celestial bodies and terrestrial bodies, but the glory of the celestial body is one, and the glory of the terrestrial is another. There is a natural (human) body and there is a spiritual body.

In this book, I will address two of these bodies...the spiritual and natural (human). That which is spiritual was not first but that which is natural.

"And as we have borne the image of the earthy, we shall also bear the image of the heavenly."

This little book is a parallel of the spiritual body and the natural (or human) body. The human body takes on the characteristics of the spiritual body as it aligns with the spirit. The human body is a complex collection of individual living units called cells. Human beings begin life as a single cell. Each cell has the ability to reproduce, exchange gases, move, react to external and internal stimuli and create or utilize energy to perform their tasks. Our natural bodies consist of many members. Each part is made to perform a certain function(s), like as unto the cell. Individually, each member is limited in what it can do, but collectively and working together, these same individual members can accomplish so much more.

Each person is an individual. Each of us was created and gifted to do certain things. Collectively and Corporately we form a body as we come together in agreement.

As God in three is one (Father, Son and Holy Spirit), so is man in three is one (spirit, soul, and body).

The spiritual body is the image and likeness of God, our creator. The natural body is the house, carrier, earth suit of the spiritual body. Individually, we're to present our bodies as living sacrifices, holy and acceptable unto God....and collectively, we're to present ourselves as one unto God Almighty.

Let's look at the human body (some of its parts and their functions) to help us understand how we are to function as the spiritual body; the body of Christ.

Victoria R. Bradley

THE BODY/PARTS

Each part of the body is responsible for a particular function. Do you know which part you are? Are you trying to be a hand when you are a foot? Or and eye when you are an ear? Are you a healthy part of the body or a sick part of the body?

I am not permitted to list every part, but let us look at some parts of the body and their function in the following order:

THE HEAD (MIND, SOUL)	Creates, Leads, Thinks
THE EYES	See, Perceives
THE NOSE	Smells, Sniffs Out
THE MOUTH	Speaks, Tastes
THE EARS	Hears, Listens
THE NECK	Supports the Head, Connects
THE HEART	Feels, Loves
THE SHOULDER	Bears, Carries
THE ARMS	Connects the hands to the shoulder
THE HANDS	Reaches, Picks up
THE WOMB/LOIN	Receives, Carries
THE FEET	Stands, Transport
THE BONE	Provides Structure
THE SKIN	Covers, Protects

Organs within the body work together in groups known as systems. Each has their own important set of functions to perform within the body. All the systems must walk in close harmony to ensure that the body remains healthy.

THE MUSCULAR SYSTEM	THE CARDIOVASCULAR SYSTEM
THE SKELETAL SYSTEM	THE NERVOUS SYSTEM
THE ENDOCRINE SYSTEM	THE IMMUNE SYSTEM
THE RESPIRATORY SYSTEM	THE DIGESTIVE SYSTEM
THE URINARY SYSTEM	THE REPRODUCTIVE SYSTEM

I beseech you therefore, brethren, by the mercies of God, that you present your bodies a living sacrifice, holy, acceptable unto God, which is your reasonable service.

For as we have many members in one body, and all members have not the same office: so, we being many, are one body in Christ, and every one members one of another.

For as the body is one, and has many members, and all the members of that one body, being many, are one body: so, also is Christ. For by one Spirit are we all baptized into one body, whether we be Jews or Gentiles, whether we be bond or free; (whether we be black or white) and have been all made to drink into one Spirit. For the body is not one member, but many.

If the foot shall say, "Because I am not the hand, I am not of the body"; is it therefore not of the body? And if the ear shall say, "Because I am not the eye, I am not of the body"; is it therefore not of the body? If the whole body were an eye, where is the hearing? If the whole were hearing, where is the smelling? But now has God set the members every one of them in the body, as it has pleased him. And if they were all one member, where were the body? But now are they many members, yet but one body. And the foot cannot say unto the hand, I have no need of thee; nor again the head to the feet, I have no need of you. Nay, much more those members of the body, which seem to be more feeble, are necessary; and those members of the body, which we think to be less honorable, upon these we bestow more abundant honor; and our uncomely parts have more abundant comeliness. For our comely parts have no need; but God has tempered the body together, having given more abundant honor to that part which lacked; that there should be no schism in the body; but that the members should have the same care one for another. And whether one member suffer, all the members suffer with it; or one member be honored, all the members rejoice with it. Now you are the body of Christ, and members in particular.

Know you not that you are the temple of God, and that the Spirit of God dwells in you? If any man defiles the temple of God, him shall God destroy; for the temple of God is holy, which temple you are.

Romans 12:1	Ephesians 4:15-16	Matthew 5:13-14
Matthew 10:28	Colossians 2:10	1 Corinthians 12:18-27

THE HEAD
(MIND/BRAIN/SOUL)

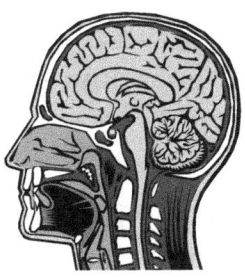

> THE NATURAL MIND
>
> Your head balances at the top of your trunk. It contains the brain, which is the body's control center. The brain is the site of consciousness, allowing us to think, create, make decisions, and initiate and control our actions.
>
> The brain is where we feel emotion such as love and anger. . It also contains sense organs that allow you to see, hear, smell, and taste. The brain is sometimes called a computer, but it is capable of creativity in a way no computer has yet achieved. It is delicate. This body-wide network reports to the central nerve system on the state of events outside and inside the body.

> THE SPIRITUAL MIND
>
> Some of us function as the head (the soul, mind, or brain) of the body so we must renew our minds daily and must possess and prosper in our souls continuously. The mind is the battlefield arena. We are the thinking part. We are charged to help keep things balanced in the body. You know how emotional we can get. The sense organs are also located in the head of the body. We will talk about them separately. In our consciousness, we are reminded to be God-conscious, not so self-conscious or world-conscious.

INSTRUCTIONS TO THE HEADS FROM THE ONE WHO IS <u>THE</u> HEAD: GOD!

And you shall love the Lord your God with all your heart and with all your soul and with all your <u>mind</u> and with all your strength; this is the first commandment.

And be not conformed to this world: but be transformed by the renewing of your <u>mind</u> that you may prove what is that good, and acceptable, and perfect will of God.

For who has known the <u>mind</u> of the Lord, that he may instruct him? Or who has been his counselor? But we have the <u>mind</u> of Christ. Let this <u>mind</u> be in you which was also in Christ Jesus (made himself of no reputation, took upon him the form of a servant, humbling himself and became obedient unto death).

Therefore, let us, as many as are mature, have this <u>mind</u>; and if in anything you think otherwise, God will reveal even this to you.

For as much then as Christ has suffered for us in the flesh, arm yourselves likewise with the same <u>mind</u>.

Let us walk by the same rule; let us <u>mind</u> the same thing. Be of the same <u>mind</u> toward one another, Do not set your mind on high things, but associate with the humble. Do not be wise in your own opinion. Be not high <u>minded</u>, but fear…

Now I beseech you, brethren, by the name of our Lord Jesus Christ, that you all speak the same thing, and that there be no divisions among you; but that you be perfectly joined together in the same <u>mind</u> and in the same judgment. Be <u>like-minded</u>, having the same love, being of one accord, of one <u>mind</u>…in lowliness of <u>mind</u> let each esteem other better than themselves….

The God of patience and consolation grant you to be <u>like-minded</u> one toward another according to Christ Jesus: that you may with one <u>mind</u> and one mouth glorify God, even the Father or our Lord Jesus Christ.

And the peace of God, which passes all understanding, shall keep your hearts and <u>minds</u> through Christ Jesus.

They that are after the flesh do <u>mind</u> the things of the flesh; but they that are after the Spirit the things of the Spirit. To be carnally <u>minded</u> is death, but to be spiritually <u>minded</u> is life and peace. Because the carnal <u>mind</u> is enmity against God; for it is not subject to the law of God, nor indeed can be. So then, those who are in the flesh cannot please God.

For God has not given us the spirit of fear, but of power, and of love, and of a sound <u>mind</u>.

"And they came to Jesus, and saw him that was possessed with the devil, and had the legion, sitting, and clothed, and in his right <u>mind</u> …"

And he that searches the hearts knows what is the <u>mind</u> of the Spirit, because he makes intercession for the saints according to the will of God. Let every man be fully persuaded in his own <u>mind</u>.

For this is the covenant that I will make with the house of Israel after those days, says the Lord: I will put my laws in their <u>mind</u>, and write them in their hearts; and I will be to them a God, and they shall be to me a people.

And even as they did not like to retain God in their knowledge, God gave them over to a reprobate <u>mind</u>, to do those things which are not convenient…

A fool utters all his <u>mind</u>: but a wise man keeps it in till afterwards.

A double <u>minded</u> man is unstable in all his ways.

Wherefore gird up the loins of your <u>mind</u>, be sober, and hope to the end for the grace that is to be brought unto you at the revelation of Jesus Christ

But their <u>minds</u> were <u>blinded</u>…in whom the god of this world have <u>blinded</u> the <u>minds</u> of them which believe not, lest the light of the glorious gospel of Christ who is the image of God, should shine unto them.

But I fear, lest by any means, as the serpent beguiled Eve through his subtility, so your <u>minds</u> should be corrupted from the simplicity that is in Christ.

For if there be first a willing <u>mind</u>, it is accepted according to what one has, and not according to what he does not have.
And be renewed in the Spirit of your <u>mind</u>…

Oh, let the wickedness of the wicked come to an end; but establish the just; for the righteous God tries the hearts and <u>minds</u>. Examine me, O Lord, and prove me; try my <u>mind</u> and my heart.

Thou will keep him in perfect peace, whose <u>mind</u> is stayed on thee; because he trusts in thee.

So, we built the wall, and the entire wall was joined together up to half its height, for the people had a <u>mind</u> to work.

Therefore, if there is any consolation in Christ, if any comfort of love, if any fellowship of the Spirit, if any affection and mercy, fulfill my joy by being like-<u>minded</u>, having the same love, being of one accord, of one mind.

I, the Lord, search the heart; I try the <u>reins</u>, even to give every man according to his ways, and according to the fruit of his doings.

Get thee behind me, Satan ; thou art an offense unto me for thou <u>mind</u> not the things that be of God, but those that be of men.

Finally, brethren, whatsoever things are true, whatsoever things are honest, whatsoever things are just, whatsoever things are pure, whatsoever things are lovely, whatsoever things are of good report; if there be any virtue, and if there be any praise, <u>think</u> on these things.

Think not that I am come to destroy the law, or the prophets; I am not come to destroy, but to fulfill. Think not that I am come to send peace on earth, I came not to send peace, but a sword.

For as he thinks in his heart, so is he…

For the word of God is living and powerful, and sharper than any two-edge sword, piercing even to the division of soul and spirit, and of joints and marrow, and is a discerner of the thoughts and intents of the heart.

Then the Lord saw that the wickedness of man was great in the earth, and that every intent of the thoughts of his heart was only evil continually.

The thoughts of the diligent tend only to plenteousness; but of every one that is hasty only to want. The thoughts of the righteous are right. Commit your works unto the Lord, and your thoughts shall be established.

Take no thought for your life, what you shall eat; what you shall drink, neither for the body, what you shall put on…neither be of a doubtful mind. For your Father knows that you have need of these things. But rather seek you first the kingdom of God; and all these things shall be added unto you. Which of you by taking thought can add one cubit unto your stature?

And when they bring you unto the synagogues, and unto magistrates, and powers, take you no thought how or what thing you shall answer, or what you shall say: for the Holy Ghost shall teach you in the same hour what you ought to say.

For I know the thoughts that I think toward you, says the Lord, thoughts of peace and not of evil, to give you an expected end.

Casting down imaginations and every high thing that exalts itself against the knowledge of God, and bringing into captivity every thought to the obedience of Christ…

The thought of foolishness is sin: and the thoughts of the wicked are an abomination to the Lord and an abomination to men.

How precious also are your <u>thoughts</u> unto me, O God! How great is the sum of them.

Curse not the king, no not in thy <u>thought</u>; and curse not the rich in your bedchamber; for a bird of the air shall carry the voice, and that which has wings shall tell the matter.

The <u>thoughts</u> of the wicked are an abomination to the Lord; but the words of the pure are pleasant words.

For from within, out of the heart of men, proceed evil <u>thoughts</u>, adulteries, fornications, murders, thefts, covetousness, wickedness, deceit, lasciviousness, an evil eye, blasphemy, pride, foolishness: all these evil things come from within, and defile a man.
Commit your works to the Lord, and your <u>thoughts</u> will be established.

Beloved, I pray that you may prosper in all things and be in health just as your <u>soul</u> prospers.
In your patience possess you your <u>souls</u>. The <u>soul</u> of the sluggard desire, and have nothing; but the <u>soul</u> of the diligent shall be made fat.

My <u>meditation</u> of him shall be sweet: I will be glad in the Lord.

Mark 12:30	Luke 10:27	Romans 12:2
Philippians 4:7-8	2 Timothy 1:7	Philippians 2:5
Romans 1:28	Romans 8:5-7	Romans 11:34
Jeremiah 29:11	2 Corinthians 10:5	Ecclesiastes 10:20
Proverbs 23:7	1 Peter 1:13	Proverbs 15:26
1 Corinthians 2:16	Psalm 7:9	Psalm 26:2
Jeremiah 17:10	Matthew 16:23	Psalm 11l:5
Romans 12:16	Psalm 104:34	Nehemiah 4:6
2 Corinthians 4:4	Ephesians 4:23	Philippians 2:2-3
James 1:8/26	Hebrews 8:10	1 Chronicles 28:9
Mark 7:21-23	Mark 8:17-18	3 John 2
Hebrews 4:12	Mark 8:33	Genesis 6:5
2 Corinthians 8:12		

JESUS CHRIST IS OUR HEAD AS WE ARE THE BODY OF CHRIST

Victoria R. Bradley

THE EYES

THE NATURAL EYE

The eye is the vision of the body, focusing, seeking, processing what is seen.

The eye is made up of many different parts that work together to help you see. The Macula provides central vision. The lens helps to focus light. The iris regulates the amount of light that enters the eye through the pupil. The pupil is the opening at the center of the iris. The cornea helps your eye focus light so things look sharp and clear. The optic nerve carries visual messages from the retina to the brain. The retina is the light-sensitive tissue that sends electrical impulses through the optic nerve to the brain. The eyelids close to keep harsh light and harmful objects out and the eyelashes help catch dust and debris before they get into your eye.

THE SPIRITUAL EYE

Some of us are eyes to the body of Christ. We need to make sure we see things through the eyes of God, not through our natural eyes. We can see what and when others can't. When there are near and far sightedness in the members, we are to be corrective to them. Light enters the body through the eye. We must be transparent in order to allow light to enter. If there is error, the images are blurred, so focus is needed.

INSTRUCTIONS FOR THE EYES FROM THE ONE WHO SEES EVERYTHING.

The <u>eyes</u> of the Lord are in every place, beholding the evil and the good. For the <u>eyes</u> of the Lord run to and from throughout the whole earth to show Himself strong on behalf of those whose heart is loyal to Him.

The <u>eyes</u> of the Lord preserve knowledge, and he overthrows the words of the transgressor.

The light of the body is the <u>eye</u>: if therefore your <u>eye</u> be single, the whole body shall be full of light. But if your <u>eye</u> be evil, your whole body shall be full of darkness.

He that has a bountiful <u>eye</u> shall be blessed; for he gives of his bread to the poor.

Be not wise in your own <u>eyes</u>: fear the Lord, and depart from evil. Let not the words of the Lord depart from your <u>eyes</u>; keep them in the midst of your heart. Let your <u>eyes</u> look right on, and let your <u>lids</u> look straight before you.

And why behold the mote that is in your brother's <u>eyes</u>, but considers not the beam that is in your own? Or how will you say to your brother, let me pull out the mote out of your <u>eye</u>, and behold, a beam is in your own <u>eye</u>? You hypocrite, first cast out the beam out of your own <u>eye</u>; and then shall you <u>see</u> clearly to cast out the mote out of your brother's <u>eye</u>.

All the ways of a man are clean in his own <u>eyes</u>; but the Lord weighs the spirits. There is a generation that are pure in their own <u>eyes</u>! And their <u>lids</u> are lifted up. Hell and destruction are never full; so the <u>eyes</u> of man are never satisfied.
He that gives unto the poor shall not lack; but he that hides his <u>eyes</u> shall have many a curse. The way of a fool is right in his own <u>eyes</u>; but he that hearkens unto counsel is wise.

Many prophets and righteous men have desired to see those things which you see, and have not seen them; and to hear those things which you hear and have not heard them.

So, the Lord said to him, "Who has made man's mouth? Or who makes the mute, the deaf, the seeing, or the blind? Have not I, the Lord? The hearing ear and the seeing eye the Lord has made even both of them. Having eyes, do you not see? And having ears, do you not hear? And do you not remember?

He who planted the ear, shall He not hear? He who formed the eye, shall He not see?

Therefore, speak I to them in parables: because they seeing see not; and hearing they hear not, neither do they understand. And in them is fulfilled the prophecy of Isaiah, which says, by hearing ye shall hear, and shall not understand; and seeing ye shall see, and shall not perceive. For this people's heart is waxed gross, and their ears are dull of hearing, and their eyes they have closed; lest at any time they should see with their eyes, and hear with their ears, and should understand with their heart, and should be converted, and I should heal them. But blessed are your eyes, for they see; and your ears, for they hear.

...the blind men came to him and Jesus says unto them "Believe you that I am able to do this?" They said unto him, "Yea, Lord." Then touched he their eyes, saying, "According to your faith be it unto you" and their eyes were opened...

For we were saved in this hope, but hope that is seen is not hope; for why does one still hope for what he sees? But if we hope for what we do not see, we eagerly wait for it with perseverance....while we do not look at the things which are seen, but at the things which are not seen. For the things which are seen are temporary, but the things which are not seen are eternal.

...providing honorable things, not only in the sight of the Lord, but also in the sight of men.

I pray that the eyes of your understanding be enlightened; that you may know what is the hope of His calling, what are the riches of the glory of His inheritance in the saints...

So, the Lord said to him, "Who has made man's mouth? Or who makes the mute, the deaf, the seeing, or the blind? Have not I, the Lord?

Blessed are the pure in heart, for they shall see God.

And the eye cannot say to the hand, "I have no need of you"; nor again the head to the feet, "I have no need of you."

For all that is in the world – the lust of the flesh, the lust of the eyes, and the pride of life – is not of the Father but is of the world.

…that whosoever looks on a woman to lust after her has committed adultery with her already in his heart. And if your right eye offends you, pluck it out, and cast it from you…

They do not know nor understand; for He has shut their eyes so that they cannot see, and their hearts, so that they cannot understand.

For My eyes are on all their ways; they are not hidden from My face; nor is their iniquity hidden from My eyes.

And Elisha prayed, and said, Lord I pray, open his eyes that he may see. Then the Lord opened the eyes of the young man, and he saw.

…To open their eyes, in order to turn them from darkness to light, and from the power of Satan to God, that they may receive forgiveness of sins and an inheritance among those who are sanctified by faith in me.

Behold the eye of the Lord is on those who fear Him, on those who hope in His mercy. The eyes of the Lord are on the righteous, and his ears are open to their cry.

Eat not the bread of him that has an evil eye, neither desire his dainty meats.

Except you see signs and wonders, you will not believe. Judge not according to the appearance, but judge righteous judgment.
The Lord hates a proud look, a lying tongue, and hands that shed innocent blood…

Victoria R. Bradley

No man has <u>seen</u> God. The only begotten son has declared Him.

And if your <u>eye</u> causes you to sin, pluck it out and cast it from you. It is better for you to enter into life with one <u>eye</u>, rather than having two <u>eyes</u> to be cast into hell fire.

All things are full of labor; man cannot express it. The <u>eye</u> is not satisfied with <u>seeing</u>, nor the ear filled with hearing.

But as it is written: <u>Eye</u> has not <u>seen</u>, nor ear heard, nor have entered into the heart of man the things which God has prepared for those who love Him. But God has revealed them to us through His Spirit…
For, now we <u>see</u> in a mirror, dimly, but then face to face.

For we walk by faith, not by <u>sight</u>.

Open my <u>eyes</u> that I may see wondrous things from Your law.

Turn away my <u>eyes</u> from looking at worthless things and revive me in Your way.

The Lord opens the <u>eyes</u> of the <u>blind</u>; the Lord raises those who are bowed down; the Lord loves the righteous.

I will instruct you and teach you in the way you should go; I will guide you with <u>My eye</u>.

He found him in a desert land and in the wasteland, a howling wilderness; he encircled him, he instructed him, he kept him as the apple of <u>His eye</u>.

You are those who justify yourselves before men but God knows your hearts. For what is highly esteemed among men is an abomination in the <u>sight</u> of God.

The light of the <u>eyes</u> rejoices the heart, and a good report makes the bones healthy.

For since the creation of the world His invisible attributes are clearly <u>seen</u>, being understood by the things that are made…

It shall be as a sign on your hand and as frontlets between your eyes, for by strength of hand the Lord brought us out of Egypt.

I will set nothing wicked before my eyes; I hate the work of those who fall away; It shall not cling to me.

I will lift up my eyes to the hills from whence comes my help. My help comes from the Lord who made heaven and earth. Unto you I lift up my eyes…

I have made a covenant with my eyes; why then should I look upon a young woman?

The lamp of the body is the eye. Therefore, when your eye is good, your whole body also is full of light. But when your eye is bad, your body also is full of darkness.

Jesus said to him, "Thomas, because you have seen Me, you have believed. Blessed are those who have not seen and yet have believed.

My friends scorn me; my eyes pour out tears to God,

He who winks with the eye causes trouble,…

But all their works they do to be seen by men…

Consider and hear me, O Lord my God: enlighten my eyes lest I sleep the sleep of death…

And do this, knowing the time, that now it is high time to wake out of sleep; for now our salvation is nearer than when we first believed

Love not sleep, lest you come to poverty; open thine eyes, and you shall be satisfied with bread. How long will you sleep, O sluggard?
When will you arise out of your sleep? Yet a little sleep, a little slumber, a little folding of the hands to sleep: so, shall your poverty come as one that travels and you want as an armed man. Watch therefore, for you know neither the day nor

the hour wherein the Son of man comes. Lest coming suddenly he find you <u>sleeping</u>. And what I say unto you I say unto all, <u>Watch</u>.

What, could you not <u>watch</u> with me one hour? <u>Watch</u> and pray, that you enter not into temptation: the spirit indeed is willing, but the flesh is weak. Why <u>sleep</u> you? Rise and pray, lest you enter into temptation.

He has <u>blinded</u> their <u>eyes</u> and hardened their hearts lest they should <u>see</u> with their <u>eyes</u>, lest they should understand with their hearts and turn, so that I should heal them.

Let them alone, they are <u>blind</u> leaders of the <u>blind</u>. And if the <u>blind</u> leads the <u>blind</u>, both will fall into a ditch,

<u>Blindness</u> in part has happened to Israel until the fullness of the Gentiles has come in.

Can the <u>blind</u> lead the <u>blind</u>? Shall they not both fall into the ditch?

…whose minds the god of this age has <u>blinded</u>, who do not believe, lest the light of the gospel of the glory of Christ, who is the image of God, should shine on them.

Behold, He is coming with clouds and every <u>eye</u> will see Him, even they who pierced Him and all tribes of the earth will mourn because of Him. Even so, Amen.

Teach Me Your Way, Oh Lord

- John 1:18/20:29
- Romans 8:24-25/13:11
- 2 Corinthians 8:21
- 1 Corinthians 2:9
- Ecclesiastes 1:8
- Matthew 15:14
- Psalm 119:18/37
- Psalm 32:8
- Psalm 121:1
- Deuteronomy 32:10
- Matthew 6:22-23 (Luke 11:34)
- Matthew 5:8
- 2 Corinthians 5:7
- 1 Corinthians 13:12
- 2 Corinthians 4:4
- Matthew 13:13-16
- Matthew 5:38
- Jeremiah 5:21
- 2 Chronicles 16:9
- 2 Corinthians 4:18
- Galatians 4:15
- Psalm 32:8
- Matthew 18:9
- Mark 8:17-18
- Ephesians 1:18/3:3
- Proverbs 20:12
- Proverbs 15:30
- Matthew 23:5
- Psalm 101:3
- 2 Kings 6:17
- Psalm 123:1
- John 20:29
- Proverbs 10:10
- Proverbs 15:3
- Job 31:1
- John 12:40
- Psalm 31:9
- Matthew 7:3-5
- Psalm 34:15
- Jeremiah 16:17
- 1 Corinthians 12:21
- Zechariah 2:8
- Proverbs 4:25/16:2
- Acts 26:18
- Psalm 33:18
- Psalm 88:9
- Job 16:20
- Romans 1:20
- Exodus 13:16
- Psalm 94:9
- Psalm 146:8
- Psalm 13:3
- Habakkuk 1:13
- John 1:9
- Deuteronomy 34:7
- Exodus 4:11
- Luke 6:41-42
- Psalm 6:7
- Matthew 5:29
- 1 John 2:16
- Mark 7:21-23
- Acts 26:18
- Isaiah 44:18
- Exodus 21:29

THE NOSE

THE NATURAL NOSE

You might not think your nose is a "vital" organ, but it is. Just have a bad cold. Nasal congestion and a runny nose have a noticeable effect on quality of life, energy level, ability to breathe, ability to sleep, and ability to function in general.

Why is your nose so important? It processes the air that you breathe before it enters your lungs. Your nose protects your health by:
- filtering all that air and retaining particles as small as a pollen grain with 100% efficiency
- humidifying the air that you breathe, adding moisture to the air to prevent dryness of the lining of the lungs and bronchial tubes
- warming cold air to body temperature before it arrives in your lungs
- nasal congestion reduces the sense of smell
- mouth breathing causes dry mouth

THE SPIRITUAL NOSE

You that function as noses are just as important to the body as any other part. What would the body do without air? Air enters and leaves the body through the nose. Mouth breathing causes dryness. We need to be moist so that other parts of the body won't become dry. The nose can sniff out bad odors and steer the body away from them.

INSTRUCTIONS TO THE NOSES FROM THE ONE THAT IS THE BREATH OF LIFE:

And the Lord God formed man of the dust of the ground, and breathed into his nostrils the breath of life; and man became a living soul.

The breath of our nostrils, the anointed of the Lord was captured in their pits, of whom we said, "Under His shadow we shall live among the nations."

But have lifted up yourself against the Lord of heaven: and have brought the vessels of his house before you, have drunk wine in them, have praised the gods of silver and gold, of brass, iron, wood, and stone, which see not, nor hear, nor know: and the God in whose hand thy breath is, and whose are all your ways, have you not glorified...

All the while my breath is in me, and the Spirit of God is in my nostrils; my lips shall not speak wickedness, nor my tongue utter deceit.

The Lord neither is worshipped with men's hands, as though he needed anything, seeing he gives to all life, breath, and all things...

For that which befalls the sons of men befalls beasts; even one thing befalls them: as the one die, so dies the other; yea, they have all one breath; so that a man has no preeminence above a beast: for all is vanity.

And with the blast of Thy nostrils the waters were gathered together, the floods stood upright as a heap, and the depths were congealed in the heart of the sea. And the channels of the sea appeared, the foundations of the world were discovered, at the rebuking of the Lord, at the blast of the breath of His nostrils.

Victoria R. Bradley

The Spirit of God has made me, and the <u>breath</u> of the Almighty has given me life.

By the blast of God they perish, and by the <u>breath</u> of His nostrils are they consumed.

But even a whole month, until it come out at your <u>nostrils</u>, and it be loathsome unto you: because that you have despised the Lord which is among you, and have wept before Him, saying "Why came we forth out of Egypt?"

All in whose <u>nostrils</u> was the <u>breath</u> of life, of all that was in the dry land, died.

The grass withers, the flower fades; because the Spirit of the Lord <u>blows</u> upon it; surely the people is grass…but the word of our God shall stand forever.

You love righteousness, and hate wickedness: therefore God, your God, has anointed you with the oil of gladness above your fellows. All your garments <u>smell</u> of myrrh, and aloes, and cassia, out of the ivory palaces, whereby they have made you glad.

If the whole body were an eye, where were the hearing? If the whole body were hearing, where were the <u>smelling</u>?

Return unto the Lord thy God…His branches shall spread, and his beauty shall be as the olive tree, and his <u>smell</u> as Lebanon.

And I will make your cities waste, and bring your sanctuaries unto desolation, and I will not <u>smell</u> the savor of your sweet odors.

And it shall come to pass, that instead of sweet <u>smell</u> there shall be <u>stink</u>; and instead of a girdle a rent; and instead of well-set hair baldness; and instead of a stomacher a girding of sackcloth, and burning instead of beauty.

I hate, I despise your feast days, and I will not <u>smell</u> in your solemn assemblies.

Thy lips, O my spouse, drop as the honeycomb; honey and milk are under thy tongue; and the smell of thy garments is like the smell of Lebanon. His cheeks are as a bed of spices, as sweet flowers; his lips like lilies, dropping sweet smelling myrrh.

And the Lord smelled a sweet savor; and the Lord said in His heart, I will not again curse the ground any more for man's sake; for the imagination of man's heart is evil from his youth; neither will I again smite any more everything living, as I have done.

Their idols are silver and gold, the work of men's hands. They have mouths, but they speak not; eyes have they, but they see not; they have ears but they hear not; noses have they, but they smell not; they have hands but they handle not; feet have they, but they walk not…they that make them are like unto them so is every one that trusts in them.

Now thanks be to God who always leads us in triumph in Christ, and through us diffuses the fragrance of His knowledge in every place. For we are to God the fragrance of Christ among those who are being saved and among those who are perishing.

But solid food belongs to those who are of full age, that is, those who by reason of use have their senses exercised to discern both good and evil.

And thou shalt burn the whole ram upon the altar: it is a burnt offering unto the Lord: it is a sweet savor, an offering made by fire unto the Lord.

But I have all, and abound: I am full, having received of Epaphroditus the things which were sent from you, an odor of a sweet smell, a sacrifice acceptable, well pleasing to God.

Let my prayer be set forth before Thee as incense; and the lifting up of my hands as the evening sacrifice.

Hear, O earth: behold I will bring evil upon this people, even the fruit of their thoughts, because they have not hearkened unto My words, nor to My law, but rejected it. To what purpose comes there to Me incense from Sheba, and the sweet cane from a far country? Your burnt offerings are not acceptable, nor your sacrifices sweet unto Me.

And when He had taken the book, the four beasts and four and twenty elders fell down before the Lamb, having every one of them harps, and golden vials full of odors, which are the prayers of saints.

Genesis 2:7/7:22	Acts 17:25	2 Corinthians 2:14-16
Lamentations 4:20	Psalm 45:7-8	2 Corinthians 2:11
Daniel 5:23	Leviticus 26:31	Hebrews 5:14
Ecclesiastes 3:19	Amos 5:21	Exodus 29:18, 25, 41
2 Corinthians 2:14-16	2 Corinthians 2:11	Hebrews 5:14
Exodus 29:18, 25, 41	Acts 10:4	Philippians 4:18
Song of Solomon 4:10-11/5:13	Jeremiah 6:19-20	Job 4:9/27:3
Isaiah 3:24	Numbers 11:20	2 Samuel 22:16
Psalm 18:15/141:2	Psalm 115:4-8	Exodus 15:8
Revelations 5:8	Job 33:4	Ezekiel 20:41
Song of Solomon 5:5/7:8, 13	Genesis 8:21	Amos 4:10
Joel 2:20	Isaiah 37:29/42:5	Daniel 3:27
Hosea 14:6	1 Corinthians 12:17	Isaiah 40:7-8

THE MOUTH
(VOICE, TONGUE, TEETH)

THE NATURAL MOUTH/TONGUE

Within the mouth are the tongue and teeth. They work together (along with other parts) to make sounds; a voice. The <u>tongue</u> is the taster – sweet, bitter, sour, salty. The teeth cuts and chews. The <u>mouth</u> is the voice of the heart and soul.

THE SPIRITUAL MOUTH/TONGUE

Some of us function as mouthpieces. We are the voice of the body. Our voice is heard. As the mouthpiece (voice), we are to speak life and not death. We are to say what our Creator says, as we agree with and believe what He says. Some time we must use our tongues in tasting to see what is good for the body and what is not. Other times we may have to cut out what is not right or chew up that which is too much for the body to digest at one time.

INSTRUCTIONS TO THE MOUTHPIECES FROM THE ONE WHO SPEAKS LIFE:

Death and Life are in the power of the <u>tongue</u>: and they that love it shall eat the fruit thereof. Man shall not live by bread alone, but by every word that proceeds out of the <u>mouth</u> of God.

The <u>mouth</u> of a righteous man is a well of life. In the <u>lips</u> of him that has understanding wisdom is found. In the multitude of words there wants not sin: but he that refrain his <u>lips</u> is wise. The <u>tongue</u> of the just is as choice silver. The <u>lips</u> of the righteous feed many. The <u>lips</u> of the righteous know what is acceptable. The <u>mouth</u> of the just brings forth wisdom, but the froward <u>tongue</u> shall be cut out.

Get wisdom, get understanding; forget it not; neither decline from the words of my <u>mouth</u>. My son, attend unto my wisdom and bow your ear to my understanding: that you may regard discretion, and that your <u>lips</u> may keep knowledge. Hear, for I will <u>speak</u> of excellent things and the opening of my <u>lips</u> shall be right things. For my <u>mouth</u> shall <u>speak</u> truth; and wickedness is an abomination to my <u>lips</u>. All the words of my <u>mouth</u> are in righteousness; there is nothing froward or perverse in them. They are all plain to him that understands and right to them that find knowledge. When you go, it shall lead you, when you sleep, it shall keep you, and when you awake, it shall <u>talk</u> with you.

Depart not from the words of My <u>mouth</u>.

A man shall be satisfied with good by the fruit of his <u>mouth</u>. A man shall eat good by the fruit of his <u>mouth</u>, but the soul of the transgressors shall eat violence.
He that <u>speaks</u> truth shows forth righteousness.

A soft <u>answer</u> turns away wrath; but grievous <u>words</u> stir up strife. The <u>tongue</u> of the wise uses knowledge aright. A wholesome <u>tongue</u> is a tree of life; but perverseness therein is a breach in the spirit.

The <u>lips</u> of the wise disperse knowledge, but the heart of the foolish does not so. A man has joy by the answer of his <u>mouth</u>; and a word spoken in due season, how good is it!

The preparation of the heart in man, and the answer of the <u>tongue</u>, is from the Lord. The heart of the wise teaches his <u>mouth</u>, and adds learning to his <u>lips</u>. Pleasant <u>words</u> are as a honeycomb, sweet to the soul, and health to the bones. The words of a man's <u>mouth</u> are as deep waters, and the wellspring of wisdom as a flowing brook.

He that keeps his <u>mouth</u> keeps his life, but he that opens wide his <u>lips</u> shall have destruction. He that has knowledge spares his <u>words</u>; and a man of understanding is of an excellent spirit. Even a fool, when he holds his peace, is counted wise: and he that shuts his <u>lips</u> is esteemed a man of understanding.

A word fitly <u>spoken</u> is like apples of gold in pictures of silver. As an earring of gold, and an ornament of fine gold, so is a wise <u>reprover</u> upon an obedient ear. He that <u>answers</u> a matter before he hears it, it is folly and shame unto him.

There is gold, and a multitude of rubies; but the <u>lips</u> of knowledge are a precious jewel. Whoso keeps his <u>mouth</u> and his <u>tongue</u> keeps his soul from troubles. Yea, my reins shall rejoice, when my <u>lips</u> speak right things.

Put away from you a false <u>mouth</u>, and perverse <u>lips</u> put far from you. You are snared (taken) with the words of your <u>mouth.</u> A naughty person, a wicked man, walks with a false <u>mouth</u>. The Lord hates a lying <u>tongue</u> and a false witness that <u>speaks</u> <u>lies,</u> and he that <u>sow</u> discord among brethren. The <u>lips</u> of a strange woman drop as a honeycomb, and her <u>mouth</u> is smoother than oil: but her end is bitter as wormwood, sharp as a two-edged sword. Lying <u>lips</u> are abomination to the Lord; but they that deal truly are his delight.

Excellent <u>speech</u> becomes not a fool; much less do lying <u>lips</u> a prince. A fool's <u>lips</u> enter into contention and his <u>mouth</u> calls for strokes. A fool's <u>mouth</u> is his destruction, and his <u>lips</u> are the snare of his soul. The <u>words</u> of a talebearer are as wounds, and they go down into the innermost parts of the belly.

Let another man praise thee, and not your own mouth; a stranger, and not your own lips. He that rebukes a man afterwards shall find more favor than he that flatters with the tongue. A man that flatters his neighbor spreads a net for his feet.

The Lord God has given me the tongue of the learned that I should know how to speak a word in season to him who is weary.

A forward man sow strife; and a whisperer separates chief friends. He that covers a transgression seeks love; but he that repeats a matter separates very friends.
A wicked doer gives heed to false lips; and a liar gives ear to a naughty tongue.
An ungodly man digs up evil; and in his lips there is as a burning fire.
Open your mouth for the dumb in the cause of all such as are appointed to destruction. Open your mouth, judge righteously, and plead the cause of the poor and needy.

The words of the wicked are to lie in wait for blood, but the mouth of the upright shall deliver them. The wicked is snared by the transgression of his lips, but the just shall come out of trouble. In the mouth of the foolish is a rod of pride: but the lips of the wise shall preserve them.

Violence covers the mouth of the wicked. He that hides hatred with lying lips, and he that utters a slander, is a fool. A hypocrite with his mouth destroys his neighbor.

The mouth of strange women is a deep pit; he that is abhorred of the Lord shall fall therein. Speak not in the ears of a fool; for he will despise the wisdom.

Where no wood is, there the fire goes out; so where there is no talebearer, the strife ceases. Burning lips and a wicked heart are like a potsherd covered with silver dross. He that hates dissembles with his lips, and lays up deceit within him.

A lying tongue hates those that are afflicted by it; and a flattering mouth works ruin. A faithful witness will not lie; but a false witness will utter lies.

Sees thou a man that is hasty in his <u>words</u>? There is more hope of a fool than of he.
The poor uses entreaties; but the rich <u>answers</u> roughly.

<u>Ask</u>, and it shall be given you; seek, and you shall find, knock, and it shall be opened unto you.

Not everyone that <u>says</u> unto me, Lord, Lord shall enter into the kingdom of heaven; but he that does the will of my Father which is in heaven.

Whosoever therefore shall <u>confess</u> me before men, him will I <u>confess</u> also before my Father which is in heaven. But whosoever shall deny me before men, him will I also deny before my Father which is in heaven.

<u>Pray</u> for them that hate you, and for them which despitefully use you, and persecute you…

Do not <u>pray</u> like the hypocrites who wants to be seen. When you <u>pray</u>, you <u>pray</u> in secret and the Father which sees in secret, shall reward you openly.
Draw me not away with the wicked, and with the workers of iniquity, which <u>speak</u> peace to their neighbors, but mischief is in their hearts.

The <u>voice</u> of the Lord makes the hinds to calve, and discovers the forests; and in his temple does everyone <u>speak</u> of His Glory.

And my <u>tongue</u> shall <u>speak</u> of your righteousness and of your praise all the day long.

My <u>mouth</u> shall <u>speak</u> of wisdom; and the meditation of my heart shall be of understanding.

The centurion answered and said, "Lord, I am not worthy that you should come under my roof; but <u>speak the word only</u>, and my servant shall be healed.

And these signs shall follow them that believe; In my name shall they cast out devils; they shall <u>speak</u> with new <u>tongues</u>.

Your tongue devise mischief like a sharp razor, working deceitfully. You love evil more than good; and lying rather than to speak righteousness. You love all devouring words, O your deceitful tongue. God shall likewise destroy you forever, He shall take you away and pluck you out of your dwelling place, and root you out of the land of the living.

He that speaks truth shows forth righteousness: but a false witness deceit.

The lip of truth shall be established for ever: but a lying tongue is but for a moment. A true witness delivers souls: but a deceitful witness speaks lies.

In the mouth of the foolish is a rod of pride: but the lips of the wise shall preserve them.

Go from the presence of a foolish man, when you perceive not in him the lips of knowledge.

Exodus 4:11	Matthew 5:44	Matthew 7:7,21
Isaiah 50:4	Matthew 8:8	Matthew 10:32-33
Mark 16:17	Matthew 15:11	Matthew 16:17
Acts 4:29	Acts 5:40	Matthew 4:4
1 Corinthians 2:6-7	James 1:26	Romans 10:10
Colossians 4:6	Ephesians 4:29	Joshua 1:8
Psalm 28:3	Psalm 35:28	Psalm 49:3
Psalm 52:3	Psalm 119:172	Proverbs 14:7
Proverbs 4:5	Proverbs 4:24	Proverbs 5:17
Proverbs 6:2/6:12	Proverbs 6:16/6:22	Proverbs 8:6-9
Proverbs 10:11/10:13	Proverbs 10:19-21, 31	Proverbs 12:6
Proverbs 12:13-14, 17-19	Proverbs 13:2-3	Proverbs 14:3,5
Proverbs 12:22	Proverbs 15:1,4,7,23,28	Proverbs 16:23-24
Proverbs 16:27	Proverbs 17:4,7-9	Proverbs 17:27-28
Proverbs 18:4,6-7	Proverbs 18:13	Proverbs 18:21
Proverbs 20:15	Proverbs 21:23	Proverbs 22:14
Proverbs 23:16	Proverbs 24:28	Proverbs 25:11-13
Proverbs 26:20-28	Proverbs 28:23	Proverbs 29:5, 20
Proverbs 31:8-9		

THE EAR

> THE NATURAL EAR
>
> The ears are organs of both hearing and balance. The ear is a very complex organ comprising of three parts: the outer, middle and inner ear. From the inner ear the auditory nerve transmits information to the brain for processing.
>
> OUTER EAR - The outer ear funnels sound from the surrounding environment into the hearing system. The shape helps us localize where sounds in the environment are coming from.
>
> MIDDLE EAR - The middle ear is that part of the ear where sound strikes the ear drum. The middle ear is connected to the throat which keeps the air pressure equal to that of the surrounding environment. A blow to the head can cause a disconnection. This will produce a dramatic hearing loss.
>
> INNER EAR - The inner ear is the delicate structure which transforms the sound vibrations into signals that are transmitted to the brain. It plays an important role

> **THE SPIRITUAL EAR**
>
> Some of us are ears in the body. We hear what others don't. Everyone does not have an ear to hear. Too often we're listening to the wrong voice. We that are ears must be tuned in to the master's frequency. Sometimes there is too much noise in the atmosphere.

Victoria R. Bradley

INSTRUCTIONS TO THE EARS FROM THE ONE WHO HEARS EVERYTHING:

I cried unto the Lord with my voice, and He <u>heard</u> me out of His holy hill.

Father, I thank Thee that Thou has <u>heard</u> Me, and I knew that Thou <u>hears</u> Me always; but because of the people which stand by I said it, that they may believe that Thou has sent Me.

Hear you therefore the parable of the sower. When any one <u>hears</u> the word of the kingdom and understands it not, then comes the wicked one and catches away that which was sown in his heart. This is he which received seed by the way side. He that received the seed into stony places, the same is he that <u>hears</u> the word, and immediately with joy receives it; yet hath he not root in himself, but endures for a while for when tribulation and persecution arises because of the word, by and by he is offended. He also that received seed among the thorns is he that <u>hears</u> the word, and the care of the world and the deceitfulness of riches choke the word and he becomes unfruitful. But he that received seed into the good ground is he that <u>hears</u> the word and understands it; which also bears fruit, and brings forth, some a hundredfold, some sixty, some thirty.

A wise man will <u>hear</u>, and will increase learning; and a man of understanding shall attain unto wise counsels. My son, <u>hear</u> the instruction of your father, and forsake
not the law of your mother, for they shall be an ornament of grace unto your head, and chains about your neck. <u>Hear</u> instruction, and be wise, and refuse it not.

For the eyes of the Lord are over the righteous, and His <u>ears</u> are open unto their prayers; but the face of the Lord is against them that do evil.
<u>Attend</u> to know understanding. Depart not from the words of my mouth.

Incline your ear unto wisdom and apply your heart to understanding. For the Lord gives wisdom: out of his mouth comes knowledge and understanding.

Now we know that God hears not sinners; but if any man be a worshipper of God and does His will, him He hears.

That we should be to the praise of His glory, who first trusted in Christ, in whom you also trusted after that you heard the word of truth, the gospel of your salvation; in whom also after that you believed, you were sealed with that holy Spirit of promise…

Hear, for I will speak of excellent things; and the opening of my lips shall be right things for my mouth shall speak truth; and wickedness is an abomination to my lips. All the words of my mouth are in righteousness; there is nothing forward or perverse in them. They are all plain to him that understands and right to them that find knowledge.

For unto us was the gospel preached, as well as unto them; but the word preached did not profit them, not being mixed with faith in them that heard it.

…Received you the Spirit by the works of the law, or by the hearing of faith?

The Lord is far from the wicked; but he hears the prayer of the righteous.

The ear that hears the reproof of life abides among the wise. He that refuses instruction despises his own soul; but he that hears reproof gets understanding.

…for that the Lord hears your murmurings which you murmur against Him: and what are we? Your murmurings are not against us, but against the Lord.

And when the people complained, it displeased the Lord; and the Lord heard it and His anger was kindled and the fire of the Lord burnt among them and consumed them that were in the uttermost parts of the camp.

A wicked doer gives heed to false lips; and a liar gives ear to a naughty tongue.

Behold, the hire of the laborers who have reaped down your fields, which is of you kept back by fraud, <u>cries</u> and the <u>cries</u> of them which have reaped are entered into the <u>ears</u> of the Lord of Sabaoth.

But blessed are your eyes, for they see and your <u>ears</u> for they <u>hear</u>.

O bless our God, you people, and make the voice of His praise to be <u>heard</u>.

They have <u>ears</u> but they <u>hear</u> not…

He that has <u>ears</u> to <u>hear</u>, let him <u>hear</u>. The hearing <u>ear</u> and the seeing eye, the Lord has made even both of them.
For not the <u>hearers</u> of the law are just before God, but the doers of the law shall be justified. But be you doers of the word and not <u>hearers</u> only, deceiving your own selves.

For the time will come when they will not endure sound doctrine but after their own lusts shall they heap to themselves teachers, having itching <u>ears</u>; and they shall turn away their <u>ears</u> from the truth, and shall be turned unto fables.

So, then faith comes by <u>hearing</u>, and <u>hearing</u> by the word of God.

Behold, the Lord's hand is not shortened that it cannot save; neither His <u>ear</u> heavy that it cannot <u>hear</u>: but your iniquities have separated between you and you God and your sins have hidden His face from you that He will not <u>hear</u>.

The Lord God has opened my <u>ear</u>…for we cannot but speak the things which we have seen and <u>heard</u>.

Therefore, whosoever <u>hears</u> these sayings of Mine, and does them, I will liken him unto a wise man which built his house upon a rock…And every one that <u>hears</u> these sayings of Mine and does them not, shall be likened unto a foolish man which built his house upon the sand.

Verily, verily, I say unto you, the hour is coming and now is when the dead shall <u>hear</u> the voice of the Son of God and they that <u>hear</u> shall live.

Verily, verily, I say unto you, He that <u>hears</u> My word and believes on Him that sent Me, has everlasting life, and shall not come into condemnation; but is passed from death unto life.

For this cause also thank we God without ceasing because when you received the word of God which you <u>heard</u> of us, you received it not as the word of men, but as it is in truth, the word of God, which effectually works also in you that believe.

To whom shall I speak and give warning, that they may <u>hear</u>? Behold their <u>ear</u> is uncircumcised and they cannot <u>hearken</u>; behold the word of the Lord is unto them a reproach; they have no delight in it.

You stiff-necked and uncircumcised in heart and <u>ears</u>, you do always resist the Holy Ghost as your fathers did, so do you.

Why do you not understand My speech? Even because you cannot <u>hear</u> My word.

He that planted the <u>ear</u>, shall He not <u>hear</u>? He that formed the eye, shall He not see?

And it shall come to pass, that before they call, I will answer; and while they are yet speaking, I will <u>hear</u>.

Those things which you have both learned, and received, and <u>heard</u>, and seen me, do; and the God of peace shall be with you.

For I tell you that many prophets and kings have desired to see those things which you see, and have not seen them and to <u>hear</u> those things which you <u>hear</u> and have not heard them.

He that <u>answers</u> a matter before he <u>hears</u> it, it is folly and shame unto him.

A wise son <u>hears</u> his father's instruction: but a scorner <u>hears</u> not rebuke.
The <u>ear</u> of the wise seeks knowledge.

<u>Hear</u> counsel, and receive instruction, that you may be wise in your latter end.

The hearing ear, and the seeing eye, the Lord has made even both of them.
Apply your heart unto instruction, and your ears to the words of knowledge. Bow down your ear, and hear the words of the wise and apply your heart unto my knowledge. Whosoever hears my sayings and does them, I will liken him unto a wise man, which built his house upon a rock – a solid foundation.

Whosoever shall not receive you, nor hear your words, when you depart out of that house or city, shake off the dust of your feet.

What I tell you in darkness, that speak you in light: and what you hear in the ear, that preach you upon the housetops. He that has ears to hear, let him hear.

Blessed are they that hear the word and keep it. He that is of God hears God's words.

The Lord God has given me the tongue of the learned that I should know how to speak a word in season to him who is weary. He awakens me morning by morning. He awakens my ear to hear as the learned; the Lord God has opened my ear to hear as the learned. The Lord God has opened my ear, and I was not rebellious, neither turned away back.

…the ear of the wise seeks knowledge.
He awakens me morning by morning. He awakens my ear to hear as the learned; the Lord God has opened my ear.

Proverbs 20:12	Psalm 94:9	Philippians 4:9
Psalm 3:4	Isaiah 65:24	John 11:41-42
Matthew 13:18-23	1 Peter 3:12	Numbers 11:1
Exodus 16:8	James 5:4	Isaiah 59:1-2
Psalm 66:18	Isaiah 1:15	Jeremiah 11:11
John 9:31	Psalm 135:17	Ephesians 1:13
Matthew 13:16	Luke 10:24	Romans 10:17
Matthew 11:15	Hebrews 4:2	Matthew 7:24-27
Luke 8:11-15	Romans 2:13	Galatians 3:2-3
1Thessalonians 2:13	James 1:22-24	Isaiah 50:5
Jeremiah 6:10	Ezekiel 12:2	Acts 7:51
2 Timothy 4:3-4	John 8:43	Acts 4:20
Hebrews 2:3	John 5:24-25	Mark 8:17-18

Victoria R. Bradley

THE NECK

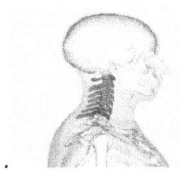

THE NATURAL NECK

The neck is the part of the body on many vertebrates that separates the head from the torso or trunk. The neck supports the weight of the head and protects the nerves that carry sensory and motor information from the brain down to the rest of the body. It contains blood vessels and nerves that supply structure in the head to the body. The neck includes part of the esophagus, larynx, trachea, thyroid and lymph nodes, and the first part of the spinal cord.

The neck is flexible and allows the head to turn and flex in all directions.

THE SPIRITUAL NECK

Some of us are just supporters. We are gifted in helping and that's all we are to do. But, we are not to suppose that support is not important. The connectors may be in the background; nevertheless, just as significant as the members out front.

INSTRUCTIONS TO THE NECKS FROM THE ONE WHO CONNECTS ALL THINGS:

My son, hear the instruction of your father, and forsake not the law of your mother, for they shall be an ornament of grace unto your head, and chains about your neck.

Let not mercy and truth forsake thee; bind them about your neck; write the upon the table of your heart, so shall you find favor and good understanding in the sight of God and man.

...nevertheless, they would not hear, but stiffened their necks, like the necks of their fathers who did not believe in the Lord their God. But they and our fathers acted proudly, hardened their necks, and did not heed your commandments...
they refused to obey...they were not mindful of your wonders that you did among them...but they hardened their necks and in their rebellion they appointed a leader to RETURN to their bondage.

Bind my commandments continually upon your heart, tie them about your neck.

Your neck is like the tower of David, built for an armory, on which hang a thousand buckers, all shields of mighty men.

So it was, when they brought out those kings to Joshua, that Joshua called for all the men of Israel, and said to the captains of the men of war who went with him, "Come ear, put your feet on the necks of these kings." And they drew near and put their feet on their necks. Then Joshua said to them, "Do not be afraid, nor be dismayed; be strong and of good courage, for thus the Lord will do to all your enemies against whom you fight."

By your sword you shall live, and you shall serve your brother; and it shall come to pass when you become restless, that you shall break his yoke from your neck.

Lose yourself from the bonds of your neck, O captive daughter of Zion!

My son, keep your father's command and do not forsake the law of your mother, bind them continually upon your heart; tie them around your neck.

But whoever causes one of these little ones who believe in Me to sin, it would be better for him if a millstone were hung around his neck, and he were drowned in the depth of the sea.

He who is often rebuked and hardens his neck will suddenly be destroyed and that without remedy.

Thus says the Lord of hosts, the God of Israel: "Behold, I will bring on this city and on all her towns all the doom that I have pronounced against it, because they have stiffened their necks that they might not hear My words."

Nevertheless, they would not hear, but stiffened their necks, like the necks of their fathers who did not believe in the Lord their God.

You stiff-necked and uncircumcised in heart and ears! You always resist the Holy Spirit; as your fathers did, so do you.

But they and our fathers acted proudly, hardened their necks and did not heed Your commandments. They refused to obey and they were not mindful of Your wonders that you did among them. But they hardened their necks and in their rebellion, they appointed a leader to return to their bondage. But You are God, ready to pardon, gracious and merciful, slow to anger, abundant in kindness, and did not forsake them. Even when they made a molded calf for themselves and said "This is your god that brought you up out of Egypt" and worked great provocations, yet in Your manifold mercies You did not forsake them in the wilderness. The pillar of the cloud did not depart from them by day to lead them on the road, nor the pillar of fire by night to show them light, and the way they should go. You also gave Your good Spirit to instruct them and did not withhold Your manna from their mouth, and gave them water for their thirst.

Forty years You sustained them in the wilderness; they lacked nothing; their clothes did not wear out and their feet did not swell. Moreover, you gave them kingdoms and nations....

Song of Solomon 4:4	Joshua 10:24	
Genesis 27:40	Isaiah 52:2	Acts 7:51
Proverbs 3:3	Proverbs 6:20-21	Matthew 18:6
2 Kings 17::14	Matthew 18:6	Proverbs 29:1
Jeremiah 19:15	Nehemiah 9:16-29	

THE HEART

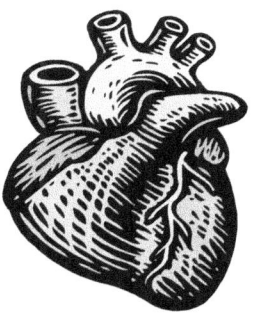

The Natural Heart

Your heart is a powerful muscle that pumps blood to every part of your body. It operates as two coordinated pumps, continuously sending blood around the body. This circulation also removes harmful wastes. The heart is linked with emotions and virtues such as love and courage. Some of us function as the heart of the body so we must keep our hearts pure.

The Spiritual Heart

Some of us function as the heart of the body. We are to pump life throughout the body. When the body loses too much blood, we are to pump blood back into that part of the body. When there is waste in the body, we remove that waste by whatever means is necessary. We were gifted with extra love that we may love on those who seem to be unlovable or those that are deeply hurting. We are to be strong for others.

INSTRUCTIONS TO THE HEARTS FROM THE HEART OF GOD:

Believe in your <u>heart</u>...Blessed are the pure in <u>heart</u> for they shall see God.

You shall love the Lord your God with all your <u>heart</u>, and with all your soul, and with all your mind, and with all your strength. This is the first and great commandment. And the second is like unto it – you shall love your neighbor as yourself.

Let your <u>heart</u> keep my commandments. Keep my commandments and live. Write them upon the table of your heart. Bind my commandments continually upon your heart. Tie them about your neck. Let your <u>heart</u> retain my words.

Keep your <u>heart</u> with all diligence; for out of it are the issues of life.

The wise in <u>heart</u> will receive commandments; but a prating fool shall fall.

Trust in the Lord with all your <u>heart</u>; and lean not unto your own understanding.

Out of the abundance of the <u>heart</u> the mouth speaks.

A good man out of the good treasure of the <u>heart</u> brings forth good things; and an evil man out of the evil treasure brings forth evil things. Thy word have I hid in my <u>heart</u> that I might not sin against thee.

Apply your <u>heart</u> unto instruction, and your ears to the words of knowledge.
Apply your <u>heart</u> to understanding. Solomon prayed for God to give him an understanding <u>heart</u> to judge his people, that he might discern between good and bad and God granted his request and more...riches and honor.

For where your treasure is, there will your <u>heart</u> be also.

Wisdom rests in the heart of him that has understanding.
A merry heart does good like a medicine. A sound heart is the life of the flesh.

The heart of the prudent gets knowledge ; and the ear of the wise seeks knowledge.

The heart of the righteous studies to answer.

The heart of the wise teaches his mouth, and adds learning to his lips.

The king's heart is in the hand of the Lord, as the rivers of water; he turns it whithersoever he will.

The preparations of the heart in man, and the answer of the tongue, is from the Lord. A man's heart devises his way; but the Lord directs his steps. Settle it therefore in your hearts, not to meditate before what you shall answer: for I will give you a mouth and wisdom, which all your adversaries shall not be able to gainsay nor resist.

For as he thinks in his heart, so is he.

Counsel in the heart is like deep water; but a man of understanding will draw it out. There are many devices in a man's heart; nevertheless, the counsel of the Lord, that shall stand. Ointment and perfume rejoice the heart; so, does the sweetness of a man's friend by hearty counsel.

Every way of a man is right in his own eyes; but the Lord ponders the hearts. He that loves pureness of heart, for the grace of his lips the king shall be his friend.

Heaviness in the heart of man makes it stoop; but a good word makes it glad.
Even in laughter the heart is sorrowful; and the end of that mirth is heaviness.

The backslider in heart shall be filled with his own ways; and a good man shall be satisfied from himself.

For this reason, I bow my knees to the Father of our Lord Jesus Christ…that Christ may dwell in your <u>hearts</u> through faith that you being rooted and grounded in love…

Then I said "I will not make mention of Him nor speak anymore in His name." But His word was in my <u>heart</u> like a burning fire shut up in my bones. I was weary off holding it back and I could not.

Then I will give them a <u>heart</u> to know Me that I am the Lord and they shall be My people and I will be their God for they shall return to Me with their whole heart.

Light is sown for the righteous and gladness for the upright in <u>heart</u>. The light of the eyes rejoices the <u>heart</u>, and a good report makes the bones healthy. But the Lord said to Samuel, "Do not look at his appearance or at his physical stature because I have refused him. For the Lord does not see as man sees for man looks at the outward appearance, but the Lord looks at the <u>heart</u>.

I know also, my God, that You test the <u>heart</u> and have pleasure in uprightness. As for me, in the uprightness of my <u>heart</u> I have willingly offered all these things.

Your word I have hidden in my <u>heart</u>, that I might not sin against You.

But, O Lord of hosts, You who judge righteously, testing the mind and the <u>heart</u>, Let me see Your vengeance on them, for to You I have revealed my cause.

And Solomon said, You have shown great mercy to Your servant David my father, because he walked before You in truth, in righteousness, and in uprightness of <u>heart</u> with You; You have continued this great kindness for him and You have given him a son to sit on his throne, as it is this day.

Therefore, give to Your servant an understanding <u>heart</u> to judge Your people, that I may discern between good and evil. And God gave Solomon wisdom and exceedingly great understanding and largeness of heart like the sand on the seashore.

Turn to Me with all your <u>heart</u>…

Then I will give them one heart, and I will put a new spirit within them, and take the stony heart out of their flesh and give them a heart of flesh…but as for those whose hearts follow the desire for their detestable things and their abominations, I will recompense their deeds on their own heads, says the Lord God.

I will put My laws in their mind and write them on their hearts and I will be their God and they shall be My people.

…that if you confess with your mouth the Lord Jesus and believe in your heart that God has raised Him from the dead, you will be saved. For with the heart one believes unto righteousness, and with the mouth confession is made unto salvation.

A high look and a proud heart, and the plowing of the wicked, is sin. Let not your heart envy sinners; but be in the fear of the Lord all the day long. As he that takes away a garment in cold weather, and as vinegar upon nitre, so is he that sing songs to a heavy heart. He that is of a proud heart stirrers up strife; but he that puts his trust in the Lord shall be made fat.

For this people's heart is waxed gross, and their ears are dull of hearing, and their eyes they have closed; lest at any time they should see with their eyes, and hear with their ears, and should understand with their heart, and should be converted, and I should heal them.

When any one hears the word of the kingdom, and understands it not, then comes the wicked one, and catches away that which was sown in his heart. This is he which received seed by the way side.

Do not let your adornment be merely outward…rather let it be the hidden person of the heart, with the incorruptible beauty of a gentle and quiet spirit, which is very precious in the sight of God.

Do not you understand that whatsoever enters in at the mouth goes into the belly, and is cast out into the draught? But those things which proceed out of the mouth come forth from the heart; and they defile the man.

For from within, out of the <u>heart</u> of men, proceed evil thoughts, adulteries, fornications, murders, thefts, covetousness, wickedness, deceit, lewdness, an evil eye, blasphemy, pride, foolishness. All these evil things come from within and defile a man.

As in water face reflects face, so a man's <u>heart</u> reveals the man.

And you will seek Me and find Me, when you search for Me will all your <u>heart</u>.

Create in me a clean <u>heart</u>, O God, and renew a steadfast spirit within me.

Delight yourself also in the Lord, and He shall give you the desires of your <u>heart</u>.

Examine me, O Lord, and prove me; try my mind and my <u>heart</u>.

Who may ascend into the hill of the Lord? ...He who has clean hands and a pure <u>heart</u>

The Lord is near to those who have a broken <u>heart</u>, and saves such as have a contrite spirit.

With my whole <u>heart</u>, I have sought you. Oh, let me not wander from Your commandments. Blessed are those who keep His testimonies, who seek Him with the whole <u>heart</u>!

Be of good courage and He shall strengthen your <u>heart</u>, all you who hope in the Lord.
My flesh and my <u>heart</u> fail; But God is the strength of my <u>heart</u> and my portion forever.

A merry <u>heart</u> does good, like medicine, but a broken spirit dries the bones.

So, teach us to number our days, that we may gain a <u>heart</u> of wisdom.

Let the words of my mouth and the meditation of my <u>heart</u> be acceptable in Your sight, O Lord, my strength and my Redeemer.

My son, do not forget my law, but let your <u>heart</u> keep my commands; for length of days and long life and peace they will add to you.

My son, give me your <u>heart</u> and let your eyes observe my ways.

Peace I leave with you; My peace I give to you; not as the world gives do I give to you. Let not your <u>heart</u> be troubled, neither let it be afraid.

For assuredly I say to you, whosoever says to this mountain, "Be removed and be cast into the sea, and does not doubt in his <u>heart</u>, but believes that those things he says will be done, he will have whatever he says.

So let each one give as he purposes in his <u>heart</u>, not grudgingly or of necessity; for God loves a cheerful giver.

...Men's <u>hearts</u> failing them for fear, and for looking after those things which are coming on the earth: for the powers of heaven shall be shaken.

And take heed to yourselves, least at any time your <u>hearts</u> be overcharged with surfeiting, and drunkenness, and cares of this life, and so that day come upon you unawares.

The <u>heart</u> is deceitful above all things and desperately wicked; who can know it? I, the Lord, search the <u>heart</u>, I try the reins, even to give every man according to his ways and according to the fruit of his doings...for the Lord sees not as man sees; for man looks on the outward appearance, but the Lord looks on the <u>heart</u>. God tries the <u>heart</u> and has pleasure in uprightness. Search me, Oh God, and know my <u>heart</u>; try me, and know my thoughts.

Say to them that are of a fearful <u>heart</u>, "Be strong, fear not; behold, your God will come with vengeance, even God with a recompense; he will come and save you.

...and He will turn the <u>hearts</u> of the fathers to the children, and He will turn the <u>hearts</u> of the children to the fathers, lest I come and strike the earth with a curse.

...from your <u>heart</u>, forgive

You are those who justify yourselves before men but God knows your hearts. For what is highly esteemed among men is an abomination in the sight of God.

Be anxious for nothing but in everything by prayer and supplication, with thanksgiving, let your requests be made known to God; and the peace of God, which surpasses all understanding, will guard your hearts and minds through Christ Jesus.

…know the God of your father, and serve Him with a loyal heart and with a willing mind; for the Lord searches all hearts and understands all the intent of the thoughts. If you seek Him, He will be found by you; but if you forsake Him, He will cast you off forever.

The heart of the righteous studies how to answer, but the mouth of the wicked pours forth evil.

Turn to me, return to the Lord your God – Rend your heart, and not your garments - For He is gracious and merciful, slow to anger, and of great kindness. Then I will give them a heart to know me, that I am the Lord, and they shall be my people and I will be their God, for they shall return to me with their whole heart.

If you will not hear and if you will not take it to heart, to give glory to My name, says the Lord of hosts, I will send a curse upon you and I will curse your blessings; yes, I have cursed them already….

…but His Word was in my heart as a burning fire shut up in my bones…

…that Christ may dwell in your hearts through faith, that you, being rooted and grounded in love….
God tries the heart and has pleasure in uprightness…

Foolishness is bound in the heart of a child; but the rod of correction shall drive it far from him. A prudent man conceals knowledge; but the heart of fools proclaims foolishness. He that troubles his own house shall inherit the wind; and the fool shall be servant to the wise of heart. Wherefore is there a price in the hand of a fool to get wisdom, seeing he has no heart to it? The foolishness of man perverts his way; and his heart frets against the Lord.

He that has a froward <u>heart</u> finds no good. They that are of a froward <u>heart</u> are abomination to the Lord; but such as are upright in their way are his delight. Before destruction, the <u>heart</u> of a man is haughty, and before honor is humility. Deceit is in the <u>heart</u> of them that imagine evil; but to the counselors of peace is joy. The Lord hates a <u>heart</u> that devises wicked imaginations. He that trusts in his own <u>heart</u> is a fool, but whoso walks wisely, he shall be delivered. O fools, and slow of <u>heart</u> to believe all that the prophets have spoken… The fool has said in his <u>heart</u> "there is no God"

….because although they knew God, they did not glorify Him as God, nor were thankful but became futile in their thoughts and their foolish <u>hearts</u> were darkened. Therefore, God gave them up to uncleanness in the lusts of their <u>hearts</u>….

Ephesians 3:17	1 Samuel 16:7	Romans 1:21, 24
1 Chronicles 29:17	Jeremiah 11:20	Jeremiah 20:9/24:7
1 Kings 3:6,9	1 Kings 4:29	Hebrews 8:10
Isaiah 35:4	Ezekiel 11:19-21	Ezekiel 36:26
Joel 2:12-13	Malachi 2:2/4:6	Matthew 5:8
Luke 1:66	2 Corinthians 3:13-16	James 1:26
Genesis 6:5	Jeremiah 17:9-10	1 Peter 3:3-4
Luke 10:27	Romans 10:10	Luke 16:15
Philippians 4:7	1 Chronicles 28:9	Mark 7:21-23
Mark 3:5	Mark 8:17-18	Mark 12:30
Proverbs 3:1-2,5	Proverbs 4:23	Proverbs 10:8
Proverbs 15:28,30	Proverbs 17:22	Proverbs 21:1
Proverbs 23:7,26	Proverbs 27:19	Jeremiah 29:13
John 14:27	Psalm 7:9	Psalm 14:1
Psalm 19:14	Psalm 24:4/26:2	Psalm 26:2
Psalm 34:18	Psalm 27:19	Psalm 31:24
Psalm 37:4	Psalm 51:10	Psalm 73:26
Psalm 90:12	Psalm 97:11	Psalm 119:1
Psalm 119:10-11	Psalm 139:23	2 Corinthians 9:7
Mark 11:23	Matthew 6:21	1 Chronicles 29:17

THE SHOULDER

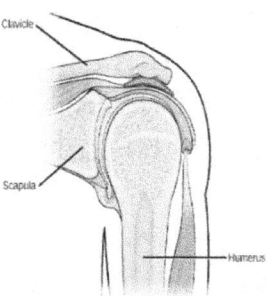

> ### THE NATURAL SHOULDER
>
> The shoulder is one of the largest and most complex joints in the body. There are important bones in the shoulder. The shoulder carries heavy loads, helps hold things together, bears responsibilities, resists.
>
> When we speak of the shoulder, we reference authority and power, subjection and servitude, oppression and cruel punishment, stubborn opposition and unwillingness, delivery and freedom.

> ### THE SPIRITUAL SHOULDER
>
> Some of us are shoulders – made to carry the burdens of those who are unable to bear them.
>
> And the government shall be upon His shoulder…Some of us help carry things that other parts of the body cannot.

INSTRUCTIONS TO THE SHOULDERS FROM THE ONE THAT BEARS US AND OUR BURDENS:

For unto us a Child is born, unto us a Son is given and the government will be upon His <u>shoulder</u>, and His name will be called Wonderful, Counselor, Mighty God, Everlasting Father, Prince of Peace. Of the increase of His government and peace, there will be no end.

And many times, You delivered them according to Your mercies, and testified against them, that You might bring them back to Your law. Yet they acted proudly and did not heed Your commandments, but sinned against Your judgments, which if a man does, he shall live by them. And they shrugged their <u>shoulders</u>, stiffened their necks, and would not hear.

Do not oppress the widow or the fatherless, the alien or the poor. Let none of you plan evil in his heart against his brother. But they refused to heed, shrugged their <u>shoulders</u>, and stopped their ears so that they could not hear.

For they bind heavy burdens, hard to bear, and lay them on men's <u>shoulders</u>, but they themselves will not move them with one of their fingers.

For every man shall <u>bear</u> his own burden. <u>Bear</u> you one another's burdens, and so fulfill the law of Christ.

For You have broken the yoke of his burden and the staff of his <u>shoulder</u>, the rod of oppressor...

It shall come to pass in that day that his burden will be taken away from your <u>shoulder</u>, and his yoke from your neck, and the yoke will be destroyed because of the anointing oil.

I removed his <u>shoulder</u> from the burden; his hands were freed from the baskets. You called in trouble, and I delivered you.

The key of the house of David I will lay on his <u>shoulder</u>; so, he shall open and no one shall shut, and he shall shut, and no one shall open.

What man of you, having a hundred sheep, if he loses one of them, does not leave the ninety-nine in the wilderness, and go after the one which is lost until he finds it? And when he has found it, he lays it on his <u>shoulders</u>, rejoicing.

Because you have pushed with side and <u>shoulder</u>, butted all the weak ones with your horns, and scattered them abroad, therefore, I will save My flock and they shall no longer be a prey; and I will judge between sheep and sheep.

They hire a goldsmith and he makes a god (from gold and silver). They prostrate themselves, yes, they worship; they bear it on the <u>shoulder</u>; they carry it and set it in its place, and it stands. From its place it shall not move, though one cries out to it, yet it cannot answer, nor save him out of his trouble.

Nehemiah 9:29	Matthew 23-4	Zechariah 7:11
Galatians 6:2	Exodus 28:12	Psalm 81:6
Galatians 6:5	Luke 15:4-5	Isaiah 22:22
Isaiah 46:6-7	Nehemiah 9:29-30	Isaiah 9:4,6
Isaiah 10:27		

THE ARM

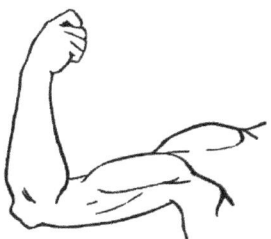

> THE NATURAL ARM
>
> The arm is the part of the upper limb between the shoulder joint and the elbow joint. The arm extends to the hand. It consists of several segments that together make it one of the most useful and complex tools of the body.
>
> The arm provides pulling and lifting strength, speed and precision while completing all kinds of movements. The arm holds, carries, assists in lifting, embraces.

> THE SPIRITUAL ARM
>
> Some of us are arms. We are used in assisting the hands. We have to hold, hug, carry, lift, push, pull, turn, stretch out in whatever way the hand dictates.

Teach Me Your Way, Oh Lord

INSTRUCTIONS TO THE ARMS FROM THE ONE THAT CARRIES US IN HIS:

...the Word of the Lord came to me saying, "Son of man, I have broken the <u>arm</u> of Pharoah King of Egypt, and see, it has not been bandaged for healing, nor a splint put on to bind it, to make it strong enough to hold a sword. Therefore, surely I am against Pharoah King of Egypt, and will break his <u>arms</u>, both the strong one and the one that was broken; and I will make the sword fall out of his hand

Therefore, say to the children of Israel: "I am the Lord, I will bring you out from under the burdens of the Egyptians. I will rescue you from their bondage,
and I will redeem you with an <u>outstretched arm</u> and with great judgments. I will take you as My people, and I will be your God. Then you shall know that I
am the Lord your God who brings you out from under the burdens of the Egyptians. And I will bring you into the land which I swore to give to
Abraham, Isaac, and Jacob: and I will give it to you as a heritage: I am the Lord."

Remember that you were a slave….and the Lord your God brought you out…by a mighty hand and by an <u>outstretched arm</u>…

For they did not gain possession of the land by their own sword, nor did their own <u>arm</u> save them, but it was Your right hand, Your <u>arm</u>, and the light of Your countenance, because you favored them.

You have scattered your enemies with your mighty <u>arm.</u>

…break the <u>arm</u> of the wicked and the evil man.

My righteousness is near; My salvation has gone forth, and My <u>arms</u> will judge the peoples; the coastlands will wait upon Me, and on My arm they will trust.

You have a mighty <u>arm</u>, strong is your hand, and high is your right hand.

With a strong hand, and with a stretched out <u>arm</u>: for his mercy endures forever.
Psalm 136:12

The eternal God is thy refuge and underneath are the everlasting <u>arms</u>, and He shall thrust out the enemy from before thee.

But his bow abode in strength and the <u>arms</u> of his hands were made strong by the hands of the mighty God of Jacob….

She girds her loins with strength and strengthens her <u>arms</u>.

The horn of Moab is cut off and his <u>arm</u> is broken, says the Lord. And from the wicked their light is withheld and the high <u>arm</u> shall be broken.

O sing unto the Lord a new song; for He has done marvelous things. His right hand and his holy <u>arm</u> has gotten Him the victory.

Hast thou an <u>arm</u> like God? Or canst thou thunder with a voice like Him?

With him is an <u>arm</u> of flesh, but with us is the Lord our God to help us, and to fight our battles.

I have made the earth, the man and the beast that are upon the ground by My great power and by My out-stretched <u>arm</u> and have given it unto whom it seemed meet unto me.

Who has believed our report? And to whom is the <u>arm</u> of the Lord revealed?

My righteousness is near; my salvation is gone forth and Mine <u>arms</u> shall judge the people; the isles shall wait upon Me and on Mine <u>arm</u> shall they trust.

The Lord has made bare His holy <u>arm</u> in the eyes of all the nations; and all the ends of the earth shall see the salvation of our God.

And even to your old age I am He, and even to hoar hairs will I carry you. I have made and I will <u>bear</u> even I will <u>carry</u> and will deliver you.

Verily, I say unto you, whosoever shall not receive the kingdom of God as a little child, he shall not enter therein. And He took them up in His <u>arms</u>, put His hands upon them and blessed them.

The heavens declare the glory of God and the firmament shows His <u>handi</u>work.

For they got not the land in possession by their own sword, neither did their own arm save them, but Thy right hand and Thine <u>arm</u> and the light of Thy countenance, because Thou had a favor unto them.

With whom My hand shall be established, Mine <u>arm</u> also shall strengthen him.

Fear and dread shall fall upon them by the greatness of Thine <u>arm</u> they shall be as still as a stone till Thy people pass over, O Lord, till the people pass over, which Thou has purchased.

Ezekiel 30:20-23	Exodus 6:6	Exodus 15:16
Psalm 10:15	Psalm 44:3	Psalm 89:10,13
Psalm 136:12	Isaiah 51:5	Psalm 19:1
Jeremiah 48:25	Deuteronomy 35:27	Proverbs 31:17
Genesis 49:24	Jeremiah 27:5	Isaiah 52:10
Mark 10:16	Psalm 89:21	Job 38:15
Deuteronomy 33:27	2 Chronicles 32:8	Psalm 98:1
Isaiah 53:1	Isaiah 46:4	Job 40:9

Victoria R. Bradley

THE HANDS (with Fingers)

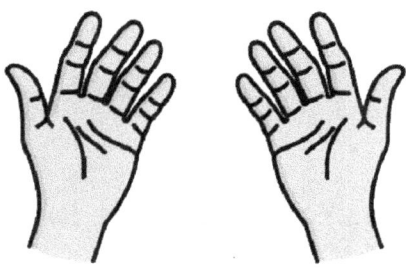

THE NATURAL HAND

The hand is the multi-fingered extremity at the end of the arm. Hands are capable of a wide variety of functions including gross and fine motor movements, pick up objects, perform heavy labor.

The hand consists of the fingers, the palm, the back, and the wrist. The hands, with the help of the fingers, nails, and arms, move, carry, lift, touch, grasp, reach, point, pull, push and pick up what is necessary.

THE SPIRITUAL HAND

The five fingers on the hand represents the five-fold ministry of God. We are His hands extended. We all can agree that without hands, life can be very difficult. Just as in the natural, the spiritual hands carry out the same functions. The hands must be available for those who are maimed or paralyzed by life's circumstances, situations, or conditions. All of us need helping hands some times.

INSTRUCTIONS TO THE HANDS FROM THE ONE IN WHO'S HANDS WE ABIDE:

When I consider Your heavens, the work of Your <u>fingers</u>…You have made us to have dominion over the works of Your <u>hands</u>…

Withhold not good from them to whom it is due, when it is in the power of your <u>hand</u> to do it.

Turn not to the right <u>hand</u> nor to the left; remove your foot from evil.

The Lord hate <u>hands</u> that shed innocent blood…

Bind the Word upon your <u>fingers</u>, write them upon the table of your heart.

He becomes poor that deals with a slack <u>hand</u>; but the <u>hand</u> of the diligent makes rich. The <u>hand</u> of the diligent shall bear rule. The desire of the slothful kills him; for his <u>hands</u> refuse to labor.

Though <u>hand</u> join in <u>hand</u>, the wicked shall not be unpunished; but the seed of the righteous shall be delivered.

Yet a little sleep, a little slumber, a little folding of the <u>hands</u> to sleep; so, shall your poverty come as one that travels and your want as an armed man.

If your <u>hand</u> or foot causes you to sin, cut it off and cast if from you. It is better for you to enter into life lame or maimed, rather than having two <u>hands</u> or two feet, to be cast into the everlasting fire.

Be strong therefore, and let not your <u>hands</u> be weak, for your work shall be rewarded.

Victoria R. Bradley

Behold, you have instructed many, and you have strengthened the weak <u>hands</u>.

God has delivered me to the ungodly and turned me over into the <u>hands</u> of the wicked.

Who shall ascend into the hill of the Lord? Or Who shall stand in his holy place? He that has clean <u>hands</u>, and a pure heart; who has not lifted up his soul unto vanity…

Yet a little folding of the <u>hands</u> to sleep; so, shall your poverty come as one that travels and thy want as an armed man.

She…work willingly with her <u>hands</u>.

The precious sons of Zion, comparable to fine gold, how are they esteemed as earthern pitches, the work of the <u>hands</u> of the potter!

For we know that if our earthly house of this tabernacle were dissolved, we have a building of God, a house not made with <u>hands</u>, eternal in the heavens.

I will therefore that men pray everywhere, lifting up holy <u>hands</u>, without wrath and doubting.

And that you study to be quiet and do your own business, and to work with your own <u>hands</u>…

Draw nigh to God, and he will draw nigh to you. Cleanse your <u>hands</u>, you sinner; and purify your hearts, you double-minded.

And now art thou cursed from the earth, which has opened her mouth to receive thy brother's blood from thy <u>hand</u>…

With a strong <u>hand</u>, and with a stretched-out arm: for his mercy endures forever.

The heaven is My throne, and the earth is My footstool: where is the house that you build unto Me? And where is the place of My rest? For all those things has Mine <u>hand</u> made, and all those things have been, says the Lord…

And behold the angel of the Lord came upon him…and he smote Peter on the side and raised him up saying, "Arise up quickly" and the chains fell off from his hands.

The heavens declare the glory of God and the firmament shows His handy work.

In His hand are the deep places of the earth; the strength of the hills is His also.

The sea is His and He made it and His hands formed the dry land.
The Lord will perfect that which concerns me. Thy mercy, O Lord, endures forever; forsake not the works of Thine own hands.

My times are in Thy hand; deliver me from the hands of mine enemies and from them that persecute me.

He teaches my hands to war so that a bow of steel is broken by mine arms. You have also given me the shield of Your salvation and Your right hand has held me up and Your gentleness has made me great.

O sing unto the Lord a new song for He has done marvelous things; His right hand and His holy arm has gotten Him the victory. You have a mighty arm. Strong is Your hand and high is Your right hand.

The voice of rejoicing and salvation is in the tabernacles of the righteous; the right hand of the Lord does valiantly. The right hand of the Lord is exalted, the right hand of the Lord does valiantly.

Remove Your stroke away from me; I am consumed by the blow of Your hand.

Arise, O Lord, O God, lift up Your hand; forget not the humble.

Send Thine hand from above; rid me and deliver me out of great waters; from the hand of strange children whose mouth speaks vanity and their right hand is a right hand of falsehood. Though I walk in the midst of trouble You will revive me. You shall stretch forth Your hand against the wrath of mine enemies and Your right hand shall save me.

I have set the Lord always before me because He is at my right hand. I shall not be moved.

If I take the wings of the morning and dwell in the uttermost parts of the sea, even there shall Your hand lead me and Your right hand shall hold me.

The Lord is my keeper. The Lord is my shade upon my right hand.

And all the inhabitants of the earth are reputed as nothing and He does according to His will in the army of heaven and among the inhabitants of the earth; and none can stay His hand or say unto Him, What doest Thou?

And remember that you were a servant in the land of Egypt and that the Lord your God brought you out from there through a mighty hand and by a stretched-out arm…

Speak comfortably to Jerusalem and cry unto her that her warfare is accomplished, that her iniquity is pardoned; for she has received of the Lord's hand double for all her sins.

In that day shall Egypt be like unto women and it shall be afraid and fear because of the shaking of the hand of the Lord of hosts which He shakes over it.

And I am sure that the king of Egypt will not let you go, no, not by a mighty hand. And I will stretch out My hand and smite Egypt with all My wonders which I will do in the midst thereof and after that he will let you go.

I the Lord have called you in righteousness and will hold your hand and will keep you and give you for a covenant of the people, for a light of the Gentiles.

O house of Israel, cannot I do with you as this potter? says the Lord. Behold, the clay is in the potter's hand, so are you in My hand, O house of Israel.

Wherefore lift up the hands which hang down and the feeble knees…

And He took them up (the little children) in His arms, put His hands upon them, and blessed them.

My Father, which gave them to Me is greater than all and no man is able to pluck them out of My Father's <u>hand</u>.

Who has measured the waters in the hollow of His <u>hand</u>, and meted out heaven with the span, and comprehended the dust of the earth in a measure, and weighed the mountains in scales, and the hills in a balance?

Mine <u>hand</u> also has laid the foundation of the earth and My right <u>hand</u> has spanned the heavens; when I call unto them they stand up together.

Both riches and honor come of Thee and Thou reigns over all and in Thine <u>hand</u> is power and might and in Thine <u>hand</u> it is to make great and to give strength unto all.

And Jabez called on the God of Israel saying Oh that Thou would bless me indeed and enlarge my territory and that Thine <u>hand</u> might be with me and that Thou would keep me from evil; that it may not grieve me. And God granted him that which he requested.

Then the Lord put forth His <u>hand</u> and touched my mouth. And the Lord said unto me, Behold I have put My words in thy mouth.

The <u>hand</u> of the Lord was upon me and carried me out in the Spirit of the Lord, and set me down in the midst of the valley which was full of bones…

Thou shalt also be a crown of glory in the <u>hand</u> of the Lord and a royal diadem in the <u>hand</u> of thy God.

I have spread out My <u>hands</u> all the day unto a rebellious people which walk in a way that was not good, after their own thoughts…

Humble yourselves therefore under the mighty <u>hand</u> of God that He may exalt you in due time.

The king's heart is in the <u>hand</u> of the Lord; as the rivers of water. He turns it wherever He will.

Because they regard not the works of the Lord, nor the operation of His <u>hands</u>, He shall destroy them and not build them up.

The Lord said unto my Lord, Sit Thou at My right <u>hand</u> until I make thine enemies thy footstool

Who is He that condemns? It is Christ that died, yea rather, that is risen again who is even at the right <u>hand</u> of God, who also makes intercession for us.

Acts 7:49-50	Acts 12:7	Daniel 4:35
Deuteronomy 5:15	Jeremiah 15:6	Jeremiah 18:6
Isaiah 48:13	Isaiah 40:2, 12	Isaiah 42:6
Isaiah 19:16	1 Chronicles 29:12	Hebrews 12:12
Mark 10:16	Exodus 3:19-20	John 10:29
Romans 8:34	Isaiah 62:13	Hebrews 1:3
1 Chronicles 4:10	Jeremiah 1:9	Ezekiel 37:1
1 Peter 5:6	Proverbs 21:1	Isaiah 65:2
Psalm 8:3	Psalm 10:12	Psalm 16:8
Psalm 18:34-35	Psalm 19:1	Psalm 28:5
Psalm 31:15	Psalm 39:10	Psalm 89:13
Psalm 95:4-5	Psalm 98:1	Psalm 110:1
Psalm 118:15-16	Psalm 121:5	Psalm 138:7-8
Psalm 139:9-10	Psalm 144:7-8	Mark 9:43
Matthew 18:8		

THE WOMB/LOINS

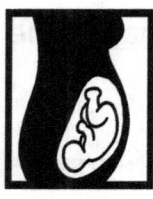

THE NATURAL WOMB
The seat of strength and vigor; the center of procreation power; a part of the body girded about and needful of covering. The uterus is super strong. It's the strongest muscle in the body by weight. It is multiple layers of tissue that run in every direction. Incredibly flexible; organic, grows a placenta; grows humans.

THE SPIRITUAL WOMB

Some of us are wombs. We carry and nurse the babies in the body. We are gifted with mother intuition and we help produce fruit that remain.

Victoria R. Bradley

INSTRUCTIONS TO THE WOMB FROM OUR CREATOR AND MAKER:

Blessed is the womb that bore you…..

The fruit of the womb is a reward

He will also be filled with the Holy Spirit, even from his mother's womb.

And it came to pass that when Elisabeth heard the salutation of Mary, the babe leaped in her womb and Elisabeth was filled with the Holy Spirit and she spake out with a loud voice and said, Blessed art thou among women and blessed is the fruit of thy womb.

And a certain man lame from his mother's womb was carried…
And a certain man was crippled from his mother's womb, who had never walked…

And not being weak in faith, he did not consider his own body, already dead (since he was about a hundred years old) and the deadness of Sarah's womb. He did not waver at the promise of God through unbelief….

God…separated me from my mother's womb and called me through His grace.

….for the Lord had closed up all the wombs of the house of Abimelech because of Sarah….

Shall I bring to the birth and not cause to bring forth? says the Lord; shall I cause to bring forth and shut the womb? says thy God.

Teach Me Your Way, Oh Lord

Before I formed thee in the belly, I knew thee and before thou came forth out of the womb, I sanctified thee and I ordained thee a prophet unto the nations.

And God said unto him, I am God Almighty. Be fruitful and multiply; a nation and a company of nations shall proceed from you, and kings shall come out of thy loins…

Gird up your loins like a man for I will demand of thee and answer thou me…

For my loins are filled with a loathsome disease and there is no soundness in my flesh.

Stand therefore, having your loins girt about with truth…a part of the whole armor of God….

…gird up the loins of your mind, be sober and hope to the end for the grace that is to be brought unto you at the revelation of Jesus Christ.

For Thou has possessed my reins. Thou has covered me in my mother's womb. I will praise The for I am fearfully and wonderfully made…My praise shall be continually of Thee.

I was cast upon Thee from the womb; Thou art my God from my mother's belly.

Behold, I was shaped in iniquity and in sin did my mother conceive me.

The wicked are estranged from the womb; they go astray as soon as they be born, speaking lies…

Jesus answered and said unto him, Verily, verily I say unto thee, Except a man be born again, he cannot see the kingdom of God. Nicodemus says unto Him, How can a man be born when he is old? Can he enter the second time into his mother's womb and be born?

And when the Lord saw that Leah was hated, He opened her womb, but Rachel was barren…And God remembered Rachel and God hearkened to her and opened her womb.

Even by the God of thy father, who shall help thee and by the Almighty who shall bless thee with blessings of heaven above, blessings of the deep that lieth under, blessings of the breasts and of the <u>womb</u>...

And the Lord spake unto Moses, saying, sanctify unto Me all the firstborn, whatever opens the <u>womb</u> among the children of Israel, both of man and of beast: it is Mine.
But unto Hannah he gave a worthy portion for he loved Hannah, but the Lord had shut up her <u>womb</u>.

And He will love thee and bless thee, and multiply thee. He will also bless the fruit of thy <u>womb</u> and the fruit of thy land, thy corn and thy wine and thine oil, the increase of thy kine and the flocks of thy sheep in the land which He sware unto thy fathers to give thee.

As for Ephraim, their glory shall fly away like a bird from the birth and from the <u>womb</u> and from the conception.

For behold the days are coming in the which they shall say, Blessed are the barren and the <u>wombs</u> that never bare and the paps which never gave suck.

And it came to pass as He spake these things, a certain woman of the company lifted up her voice and said unto Him, Blessed is the <u>womb</u> that bare Thee and the paps which Thou has sucked. But He said, Yea rather, blessed are they that hear the word of God and keep it.

Luke 11:27	Psalm 127:3-5	Psalm 139:13
Luke 1:15	Acts 3:2/14:8	Psalm 22:10
Romans 4:19-21	Galatians 1:15	Psalm 58:3
Genesis 20:18	Job 38:3	Psalm 71:6
Psalm 38:7	Ephesians 6:14	Psalm 51:5
Isaiah 66:9	Jeremiah 1:5	John 3:3-4
Genesis 29:31	Exodus 13:1-2	Hosea 9:11
Genesis 30:22	1 Samuel 1:5	Genesis 49:25
Deuteronomy 7:13	Luke 11:27-28	Luke 23:29
Job 1:21		

THE FEET

THE NATURAL FEET

The feet are so very important. They carry the entire body wherever it needs to go.

The feet are flexible structures of bones, joints, muscles, and soft tissues that let us stand upright and perform activities like walking, running, and jumping. The feet is divided into 3 sections – the forefoot, midfoot, and hindfoot.

THE SPIRITUAL FEET

Some of us are feet. We are to carry the body around. We may feel lesser because we are on the bottom part of the body, but we are just as important as every other part of the body. Think about it, the body has difficulty getting around without the feet.

INSTRUCTIONS TO THE FEET FROM OUR TRUE FOUNDATION:

How beautiful upon the mountains are the <u>feet</u> of him who brings good news, who proclaims peace, who brings glad tidings of good things, who proclaim salvation, who says to Zion "Your God reigns!"

Blessed is the man that <u>walks</u> not in the counsel of the ungodly, nor <u>stands</u> in the way of the sinners, not sits in the seat of the scornful...

My son, <u>walk</u> not in the way with sinners; refrain your <u>feet</u> from their path for their <u>feet</u> run to evil and make haste to shed blood. <u>Walk</u> in the way of good men, and keep the paths of the righteous.

My son, keep knowledge, wisdom, and understanding; then shall you <u>walk</u> in your way safely and your <u>foot</u> shall not stumble. For the Lord shall be your confidence, and shall keep your <u>foot</u> from being taken. When you go, your <u>steps</u> shall not be straightened; and when you <u>run</u>, you shall not stumble.

Ponder the path of your <u>feet</u>, and let all your ways be established. Turn not to the right hand nor to the left; remove your <u>foot</u> from evil.

The Lord hates <u>feet</u> that be swift in running to mischief. He that hastens with his <u>feet</u> sins.

He that <u>walk</u> uprightly <u>walks</u> surely; He that <u>walk</u> with wise men shall be wise; but a companion of fools shall be destroyed. He that <u>walk</u> in his uprightness fears the Lord.

Better is the poor that <u>walks</u> in his integrity, than he that is perverse in his lips, and is a fool. The just man <u>walks</u> in his integrity; his children are blessed after him.

See a man diligent in his business? He shall <u>stand</u> before kings; He shall not <u>stand</u> before mean men.

Withdraw your <u>foot</u> from your neighbor's house; lest he be weary of you, and so hate you. Whoso <u>walk</u> upright shall be saved.

A house divided against itself cannot <u>stand</u>.

Whosoever will not receive you, when you go out of that city, shake off the very dust from your <u>feet</u> for a testimony against them.

Rise, take up your bed, and <u>walk</u>.

If your hand or <u>foot</u> causes you to sin, cut it off and cast if from you. It is better for you to enter into life lame or maimed, rather than having two hands or two <u>feet</u>, to be cast into the everlasting fire.

For He must reign till He has put all enemies under His <u>feet</u>...
You have put all things under our <u>feet</u>....

Of how much sorer punishment suppose ye, shall he be thought worthy who has trodden underfoot the Son of God and has counted the blood of the covenant, wherewith he was sanctified, an unholy thing and has done despite unto the Spirit of grace?

Then they went out to see what was done and came to Jesus and found the man out of whom the devils departed, sitting at the <u>feet</u> of Jesus, clothed and in his right mind and they were afraid.

And she had a sister called Mary which also sat at Jesus' <u>feet</u> and heard His word.

And behold a woman in the city which was a sinner, when she knew that Jesus sat at meat in the Pharisee's house, brought an alabaster box of ointment; and stood at His <u>feet</u> behind Him weeping and began to wash His <u>feet</u> with tears and did wipe them with the hairs of her head, and kissed His <u>feet</u>, and anointed them with the ointment.

And He turned to the woman and said unto Simon, See thou this woman? I entered into thine house, thou gave Me no water for My feet, but she has washed My feet with tears and wiped them with the hairs of her head. Thou gave Me no kiss, but this woman since the time I came in has not ceased to kiss My feet. My head with oil thou did not anoint, but this woman has anointed My feet with ointment. Wherefore I say unto thee, her sins which are many are forgiven for she loved much but to whom little is forgiven the same loves little.

And whoever shall not receive you nor hear your words when you depart out of that house or city, shake off the dust of your feet for a testimony against them.

Heaven is My throne and earth is My footstool: what house will ye build Me? says the Lord or what is the place of My rest?

And he took him by the right hand and lifted him up and immediately his feet and ankle bones received strength, and he leaping up stood and walked and entered with them into the temple – walking and leaping and praising God.

And the God of peace shall bruise Satan under your feet shortly. The grace of our Lord Jesus Christ be with you. Amen.

Thy raiment waxed not old upon thee, neither did thy foot swell, these forty years.

And Moses sware on that day, saying, Surely the land whereon thy feet have trodden shall be thine inheritance and thy children's forever because thou has wholly followed the Lord my God…

God is my strength and power and He makes my way perfect. He makes my feet like hinds' feet and sets me upon my high places.

And he forsook the Lord God of his fathers and walked not in the way of the Lord.

If I have walked with vanity or if my foot has hasted to deceit, let me be weighed in an even balance that God may know mine integrity.

Thou made him to have dominion over the works of Thy hands; Thou has put all things under his <u>feet</u>.

He shall subdue the people under us and the nations under our <u>feet</u>.

The Lord said unto my Lord, sit Thou at My right hand until I make Thine enemies Thy <u>footstool</u>.

Let not the <u>foot</u> of pride come against me and let not the hand of the wicked remove me. There are the workers of iniquity fallen; they are cast down and shall not be able to rise.

Hold up my goings in Thy paths that my <u>footsteps</u> slip not. The law of his God is in his heart; none of his <u>steps</u> shall slide. Our heart is not turned back, neither have our <u>steps</u> declined from Thy way.

For Thou has delivered my soul from death; wilt not Thou deliver my <u>feet</u> from falling that I may walk before God in the light of the living?
I have refrained my <u>feet</u> from every evil way that I might keep Thy word.

Blessed is the man that <u>walks</u> not in the counsel of the ungodly, nor <u>stands</u> in the way of sinners, not sits in the seat of the scornful...

He brought me up also out of a horrible pit out of the miry clay and set my <u>feet</u> upon a rock and established my goings.

Ponder the path of thy <u>feet</u> and let all thy ways be established. Turn not to the right hand nor to the left; remove thy <u>foot</u> from evil.

<u>This the Lord hates</u>: A heart that devises wicked imaginations, <u>feet</u> that be swift in running to mischief...Their <u>feet</u> run to evil and they make haste to shed innocent blood; their thoughts are thoughts of iniquity; wasting and destruction are in their paths.

My son, walk not thou in the way with them; refrain thy <u>foot</u> from their path.

Victoria R. Bradley

Keep thy <u>foot</u> when thou go to the house of God and be more ready to hear than to give the sacrifice of fools for they consider not that they do evil. Be not rash with thy mouth and let not thine heart be hasty to utter anything before God for God is in heaven and thou upon earth; therefore, let thy words be few.

And how shall they preach, except they be sent? As it is written, How beautiful are the <u>feet</u> of them that preach the gospel of peace and bring glad tidings of good things!

Wherefore take unto you the whole armor of God that you may be able to withstand in the evil day and having done all, to <u>stand</u>. <u>Stand</u> therefore, having your loins girt about with truth and having on the breastplate of righteousness, and your <u>feet</u> shod with the preparation of the gospel of peace…

For He has put all things under His <u>feet</u>…

1 Corinthians 15:27	Hebrews 10:29	Luke 8:35
Romans 10:15	Proverbs 4:26-27	Luke 7:37-38
Ephesians 6:13,15	Deuteronomy 8:4	Luke 10:39
Ecclesiastes 5:1	Joshua 14:9	Acts 7:49
Romans 16:20	Luke 7:44-47	Acts 3:7
Isaiah 59:7	2 Kings 21:22	Job 31:5
Matthew 18:8	2 Samuel 22:34	Nahum 1:15
Luke 9:5	1 Corinthians 15:27	
Psalm 1:1	Psalm 8:6	Psalm 17:5
Psalm 18:33	Psalm 36:11-12	Psalm 37:31
Psalm 40:2	Psalm 44:18	Psalm 56:13
Psalm 110:1	Psalm 119:101	

THE BONES

THE NATURAL BONES

The bone is the internal framework of the body. It is a type of connective tissue that is as strong as steel but as light as aluminum. It continually breaks down and rebuilds renewing its shape and proportion during the growing process and after injury.

The function of the skeleton are to provide support, give our bodies shape, provide protection to other systems and organs of the body, provide attachments for muscles, to produce movement and to produce red blood cells.

Bones are strong enough to support weight and light enough to enable movement. Bones also offer protection to internal organs and store needed minerals. Living bones are moist.

THE SPIRITUAL BONES

The bones connect together to form the frame of the body. The bones support the weight that the body is carrying because many times the body must bear the burdens of the weak. Just like the natural bones, they are light enough for movement when the body has to move about to get things done. Some of us are protectors of the inner organs. Are you called to be living bones?

Victoria R. Bradley

INSTRUCTIONS TO THE STRUCTURAL FRAMEWORK OF THE BODY FROM THE SOLID FOUNDATION:

He keeps all his <u>bones</u>; not one of them is broken.

For these things were done, that the scripture should be fulfilled, A <u>bone</u> of him shall not be broken.

And Adam said, "This is now <u>bone</u> of my <u>bones</u>, and flesh of my flesh: she shall be called Woman, because she was taken out of Man."

Behold my hands and my feet, that it is I myself: handle me, and see for a spirit has not flesh and <u>bones</u>, as you see me have.

And Laban said to him, Surely thou art my <u>bone</u> and my flesh. And he abode with him the space of a month.

Then all Israel gathered themselves to David unto Hebron, saying, Behold, we are thy <u>bone</u> and thy flesh.

For whatsoever man he be that has a blemish, he shall not approach...Or a man that <u>is broken-footed or broken-handed...</u>

All my <u>bones</u> shall say, Lord, who is like unto thee, which delivers the poor from him that is too strong for him, yes, the poor and the needy from him that spoils him?

There were they in great fear, where no fear was: for God has scattered the <u>bones</u> of him that encamps against thee; thou has put them to shame, because God has despised them.

A virtuous woman is a crown to her husband: but she that makes ashamed is as rottenness in his bones.

The light of the eyes rejoices the heart: and a good report makes the bones fat.
A merry heart doeth good like a medicine: but a broken spirit dries the bones.

By faith, Joseph, when he died, made mention of the departing of the children of Israel; and gave commandment concerning his bones. And Joseph took an oath of the children of Israel, saying, God will surely visit you, and you shall carry up my bones from hence.

I may tell all my bones; they look and stare upon me.

At that time, saith the Lord, they shall bring out the bones of the kings of Judah, and the bones of his princes, and the bones of the priests, and the bones of the prophets, and the bones of the inhabitants of Jerusalem, out of their graves, and they shall spread them before the sun, and the moon, and all the host of heaven, whom they have loved, and whom they have served, and after whom they have walked, and whom they have sought, and whom they have worshipped…

And I will lay the dead carcasses of the children of Israel before their idols, and I will scatter your bones round about your altars.

The hand of the Lord was upon me and carried me out in the Spirit of the Lord and set me down in the midst of the valley which was full of bones…Ezekiel 37:1-11

And Elisha died, and they buried him. And the bands of the Moabites invaded the land at the coming in of the year. And it came to pass, as they were burying a man, that, behold, they spied a band of men; and they cast the man into the sepulcher of Elisha: and when the man was let down, and touched the bones of Elisha, he revived, and stood up on his feet.

As thou knows not what is the way of the spirit, nor how the bones do grow in the womb of her that is with child: even so thou knows not the works of God who makes all.

Who hate the good, and love the evil; who pluck off their skin from off them, and their flesh from off their <u>bones</u>; who also eat the flesh of my people, and flay their skin from off them; and they break their bones, and chop them in pieces, as for the pot, and as flesh within the caldron.

When I heard, my belly trembled; my lips quivered at the voice: rottenness entered into my <u>bones</u>, and I trembled in myself….

Woe unto you, scribes and Pharisees, hypocrites! For you are like unto whited sepulchers which indeed appear beautiful outside, but are within full of dead men's <u>bones</u>, and of all uncleanness.

By reason of the voice of my groaning my <u>bones</u> cleave to my skin.

Psalm 34:20
Psalm 22:17
Genesis 2:23
1 Chronicles 11:1
Proverbs 15:30
Jeremiah 8:1-3
2 Kings 13:20-21
Habakkuk 3:16
Exodus 13:19
1 Kings 13:31
Acts 9:31

Psalm 35:10
Psalm 102:5
Genesis 29:14
Leviticus 21:18-19
Genesis 50:25
Ezekiel 6:5
Ecclesiastes 11:5
Matthew 23:27
Ezekiel 24:4, 10
Job 19:20/30:30
Genesis 2:23

Psalm 53:5
John 19:36
Luke 24:39
Proverbs 12:14
Hebrews 11:72
Ezekiel 37:1-11
Micah 3:2-3
Proverbs 17:22
Joshua 24:32
Psalm 102:5

THE SKIN

THE NATURAL SKIN

The skin is the body's protective outer boundary. It is self repairing and is essential in regulating body temperature. The skin helps reveal signs of a wide range of disorders.

The skin is an organ that covers the body's entire surface protecting it from injury and infection. It is waterproof and contains a dark pigment which protects against damage from strong sunlight. The skin helps control body temperature (by sweating) and special nerve endings designed to detect touch, heat, cold, and pain.

THE SPIRITUAL SKIN

Some of us are called to be the skin of the body. God uses us to protect the outer body, covering all parts of the visible body. We help to control the temper of the body so the body does not get stuck in heat, cold, pain.

Victoria R. Bradley

INSTRUCTIONS TO THE SKIN FROM THE ONE WHO COVERS US ALL.

Thou has clothed me with <u>skin</u> and flesh, and has fenced me with bones and sinews.

And Satan answered the Lord, and said, <u>Skin</u> for <u>skin</u>, yea, all that a man has will he give for his life. But put forth thine hand now, and touch his bone and his flesh, and he will curse thee to thy face.

My bone cleaves to my <u>skin</u> and to my flesh, and I am escapes with the skin of my teeth.

My <u>skin</u> is black upon me, and my bones are burned with heat.

My flesh is clothed with worms and clouds of dust; my <u>skin</u> is broken and become loathsome.

It shall devour the strength of his <u>skin</u>; even the first-born of death shall devour his strength.

And I will lay sinews upon you, and will bring up flesh upon you, and cover you with <u>skin</u>, and put breath in you, and you shall live, and you shall know that I am the Lord.

Who hate the good, and love the evil; who pluck off their <u>skin</u> from off them, and their flesh from off their bones; who also eat the flesh of my people, and flay their skin from off them; and they break their bones, and chop them in pieces, as for the pot, and as flesh within the caldron.

By reason of the voice of my groaning my bones cleave to my skin.

And Jesus put forth his hand, and touched him, saying, I will, be thou clean. And immediately the leprosy was cleansed.

Can the Ethiopian change his skin, or the leopard his spots? then may you also do good, that are accustomed to do evil.

And though after my skin worms destroy this body, yet in my flesh shall I see God…

My flesh and my skin has he made old; he has broken my bones.

Our skin was black like an oven, because of the terrible famine.

Job 10:11	Job 2:4-5	Job 19:20
Job 30:30	Job 7:5	Job 18:13
Job 19:26-27	Ezekiel 37:6	Micah 3:2-3
Jeremiah 13:23	Lamentations 3:4	Lamentations 5:10
Luke 5:12-13	Psalm 102:5	Leviticus 13:1-11
Leviticus 22:4	2 Kings 5:26-27	Numbers 4:8-14
2 Chronicles 26:19-20	Numbers 5:2-3	Numbers 12:10-11
Matthew 8:3	Mark 1:40-42	

THE INNER PARTS

THE SYSTEMS THAT MAKE UP THE INNER BODY

The individual members are sometimes collectively connected to carry out certain functions.

THE MUSCULAR SYSTEM

The main function of muscles is to provide movement. The muscles provide coordination and structure for the body. It takes a lot of work for muscles to pull on bones so that you can move. Along with muscles and joints, bones are responsible for you being able to move. Your muscles are attached to bones. When muscles contract, the bones to which they are attached set as levers and cause various body parts to move.

The muscle has the ability to contract, to relax, to be excited by a stimulus, and to return to their original size and shape. The muscles keep the s in focus. They are capable of self-repair. If one is partly destroyed, the remaining part will grow larger and stronger in an effort to compensate.

THE CARDIOVASCULAR SYSTEM

The cardiovascular system is most basic function is to pump blood around the body. All body organs and tissues need a supply of oxygenated blood and the removal of waste products.

THE SKELETAL SYSTEM

This system forms the body's supporting framework. Joints between bones allow the skeleton to move. Some bones protect delicate internal organs.

THE NERVOUS SYSTEM

This system is the body's chief control system. It receives information and sends out instructions through nerves to all parts of the body. It is the seat of both consciousness and creativity. It works with endocrine glands to monitor and maintain other systems.

THE ENDOCRINE SYSTEM

This system initiates the changes that take place at puberty and governs many of those that are associated with our overall metabolism. Produces chemical messengers called hormones

THE IMMUNE SYSTEM

The immune system's defenses help provide vital protection against infectious diseases and malfunctions of the internal systems of the body

THE RESPIRATORY SYSTEM

This system carries air into and out of the lungs. It works together with breathing muscles, carries air into and out of the lungs.

THE DIGESTIVE SYSTEM

This system breaks food down into simple substances that can be used for energy, growth and repair. A healthy digestive system depends on the proper functioning of the immune and nervous systems.

THE URINARY SYSTEM

The kidneys filter waste substance from the blood to make urine which is stored in the bladder until it is expelled from the body.

THE REPRODUCTIVE SYSTEM

Consists of sex organs that enable men and women to produce children. Male organs called testes make sperms. Female organs called ovaries make eggs. Sperm and eggs unite to create babies. This system functions for only part of the human lifespan. It is the only system that can be surgically removed without threatening a person's life.

Our growth in the spiritual man follows the same pattern as the growth in the natural man.

THE CELL – DNA (CONTROLS ACTIVITY)

THE HUMAN LIFE CYCLE

EMBRYO

FETAL DEVELOPMENT

LABOR

DELIVERY

PREGNANCY AND LABOR

CHILDBRITH

GROWTH AND DEVELOPMENT

AGING PROCESS

INHERITANCE

THE SICK BODY

They have mouths, but they do not speak
They have ears, but they do not hear
Noses they have, but they do not smell
They have hands, but they do not handle
Feet they have, but they do not walk
Nor do they mutter through their throat

Diagnosis of a Sick Body – Diseased; Rebellious, sinful, evil doers, corrupters, forsake the Lord, provoke the Holy One, gone backward.

From the sole of the foot even unto the head, there is no soundness in it; but wounds, and bruises, and putrefying sores: they have not been closed, neither bound up, neither mollified with ointment.

Isaiah 1:4-6

- Whole head sick
- Outstretched necks
- Whole heart faints from
- No soundness in it
- Rebellious, murderers
- Silver, dross/wine mixed with water
- Loves bribes, companion of thieves
- Do not defend the fatherless or consider the widow
- Adversaries – enemies
- Idols – they worship the work of their own hands
- Proud and lofty
- Stumble and fall because their tongue and their doings are against the Lord
- Brings evil upon themselves
- Do not consider the operations of His hands
- Call evil good and good evil, who put darkness for light and light for darkness, who put bitter for sweet and sweet for bitter
- Wise in their own eyes, prudent in their own sight
- Justify the wicked for a bribe/ take away justice from the righteous
- Root rotten

- Rejects the law of the Lord of hosts and despise the word of the Holy One of Israel
- Shall stumble/shall fall and be broken, be snared and taken
- Seek the dead among the living – the mediums and wizards
- No light in them
- Every man shall eat the flesh of his own arm
- Arrogant heart
- The Lord stretches out His hand against and stricken them
- It is in the heart to destroy. The Lord uncovers their secret parts.
- Run to mischief

THE HEALTHY BODY

My <u>hands</u> to reach out to a neighbor,
My <u>ears</u> to hear when you're speaking
My <u>eyes</u> to see, My <u>heart</u> to love
My <u>feet</u> to walk in your way,
I was born to serve you, Lord.

Diagnosis of a Healthy Body – Healed/whole/complete

- Wash yourself, make yourselves clean
- Put away evil
- Cease to do evil
- Learn to do good
- Seek justice
- Rebuke the oppressor
- Defend the fatherless
- Plead for the widow
- Willing & Obedient
- Called a City of Righteousness
- Called the Faithful city
- Exalt the Lord alone
- It shall be well with them
- Eat the fruit of their doings
- Hallow the Lord of Hosts
- Not troubled
- Not fearful
- Hope in God
- Seek God
- Depend on the Lord
- Trust in the Lord

The remnant makes up the body

Victoria R. Bradley

THE BODY OF CHRIST

Blessed shall be the fruit of your body or Cursed shall be the fruit of your body

Take no thought for your life, what you shall eat, or what you shall drink, nor yet for your body, what you shall put on. Is not life more than meat and the body than raiment?

And do not fear those who kill the body but cannot kill the soul, but rather for Him who is able to destroy both soul and body in hell.

Now God worked unusual miracles by the hands of Paul so that even handkerchiefs or aprons were bought from his body to the sick and the diseases left them and the evil spirits went out of them.

…Except a man be born again, he cannot see the kingdom of God.
…Except a man be born of water and of the Spirit, he cannot enter into the kingdom of God.

Knowing this, that our old man is crucified with Him, that the body of sin might be destroyed, that henceforth we should not serve sin. Let not sin therefore reign in your mortal body, that you should obey it in the lusts thereof.

For if you live after the flesh, you shall die: but if you through the Spirit do mortify the deeds of the body, you shall live.

…Now the body is not for fornication, but for the Lord, and the Lord for the body. And God has both raised up the Lord and will also raise up us by his own power. Know you not that your bodies are the members of Christ? Shall I then take the members of Christ and make them the members of an harlot? God forbid. What? Know you not that he which is joined to an harlot is one body? For two, says he, shall be one flesh. But he that is joined unto the Lord is one spirit. What? Know you not that your body is the temple of the Holy Ghost which is in you, which you have of God, and you are not your own? For you are bought with a price: therefore glorify God in your body, and in your spirit, which are God's.

But I keep under my body, and bring it into subjection: lest that by any means, when I have preached to others, I myself should be a castaway.

For we being many are one bread, and one body: for we are all partakers of that one bread.

The resurrection of the dead is sown a natural body; it is raised a spiritual body. The first man Adam was made a living soul; the last Adam was made a quickening spirit. Howbeit that was not first which is spiritual, but that which is natural; and afterward that which is spiritual. The first man is of the earth, earthy; the second man is the Lord from heaven. And as we have borne the image of the earthy, we shall also bear the image of the heavenly.

Flesh and blood cannot inherit the kingdom of God; neither does corruption inherit incorruption. We shall all be changed in a moment, in the twinkling of an eye…

For we must all appear before the judgment seat of Christ; that every one may receive the things done in his body, according to that he has done, whether it be good or bad.

The body without the spirit is dead.

Psalm 115

Wherefore should the heathen say, Where is now their God? But our God is in the heavens; He has done whatsoever he has pleased. Their idols are silver and gold, the work of men's hands. They have mouths, but they speak not, eyes have they but they see not; they have ears but they hear not; <u>noses</u> have they but they smell not; they have hands but they handle not; feet have they but they walk not; neither speak they through their throat. They that make them are like unto them so is every one that trusts in them…You that fear the Lord, trust in the Lord.

Victoria R. Bradley

The Weather of YOUR Life

THE WEATHER OF YOUR LIFE

Question: "Are you a thermometer or a thermostat?" That was the title of one of my pastor's sermons. In other words, are you an instrument for measuring temperature or are you a gauge that controls temperature? And what does that have to do with the weather?

I think I would be safe in saying that everyone of us experience different changes in our lives. Change is inevitable. As long as we live, things, circumstances, situations, and conditions will change. I was watching the weather channel on television one day and I noticed something. The different weather *forecasts* being announced related to the different forecasts of life that announces themselves to us daily. At the same time, my mind returned to that question asked by my pastor. Putting those two things together brought me to the title of this little book.

All of us experience seasonal climate changes in our lives – outwardly and inwardly. We must understand that these changes must take place. That's life, so if you experience no change, that's a sure sign of death. We respond to the many, daily, changes in the same way that we respond to the daily weather changes – we must make the necessary adjustments in dress and in how we maneuver.

Now, just because it rains does not mean that the sun has stopped shining. And, just because it's sunny, does not mean that rain won't come. In between these are mixtures, variations and extremes. Just so you'll know, and won't need to be alarmed or surprised, listen to your spiritual weather forecast – and just dress for the type of weather at the appointed time. The weather forecast helps you prepare yourself for proper dress.

In many cases, we should be able to watch the patterns of the weather and make changes ahead of time. We should be the gauge to stability and not be the instrument to instability. If we remain constant through the changes, the way we measure the temperature will decide what instrument we are.

LET'S SEE WHAT <u>THE</u> WEATHER MAN HAS TO SAY ABOUT IT:

2 Timothy 3:10-12/Psalm 34:19

But you have carefully followed my doctrine, **manner of life, purpose, faith, longsuffering, love, perseverance, persecutions, afflictions**, which happened to me…persecutions I endured, and out of them all the Lord delivered me. Yes, and all who desire to live godly in Christ Jesus will suffer persecution. Persecution is a seasonal change.

Psalm 34:19

Many are the afflictions of the righteous, but the Lord delivers him out of them all.

2 Corinthians 5:7

For we walk by faith, not by sight, and we walk in the fruit. Sometimes, we can't see the way clearly. Sometimes, it's raining so hard, we can't see and other times it gets so dark that we can't see. So, what do we do? Walk by Faith.

Galatians 5:22

But the fruit of the Spirit is love, joy, peace, longsuffering, kindness, goodness, faithfulness, gentleness, self-control…Now walking by faith in the fruit, we cannot lose.

Colossians 1:16

…All things were created through Him and for Him. We are here on purpose for to serve and glorify the Lord. If He is the creator, don't you think that He knows all about His creation?

Romans 8:28

And we know that all things work together for good for those who love God and are the called according to His purpose. Whether it's what you would call a beautiful day – all sunny and warm, or whether it's what you would call an ugly day – all dreary and cold, all of it is working together for our good and His purpose.

Hebrews 18:8

Jesus Christ is the same yesterday and today and forever. If we know that He is the same all the time, always, why would we fret or be dismayed? Yes, the weather changes but He doesn't.

Proverbs 3:5-6

Trust in the Lord with all thine heart and lean not unto thine own under-standing. In all thy ways acknowledge Him and He will direct thy paths.
If He is all knowing, all powerful and is everything at the same time, why wouldn't we trust Him? If we trust Him, why wouldn't we acknowledge Him in all our ways, since He knows the way?

Let's review some of the "outside" forecasts and compare them to some of the "inside" forecasts:

Beautiful Day - Clear skies. No clouds in sight. Low humidity. Light winds. No Fog. Some days are just like that. These are the days we would like to keep for at least 48 hours instead of 24.

Mostly Sunny – Remember, the sun never goes down. Even though it's expressed in that way (rising and setting), and it looks that way, it does not. Even behind the clouds, the sun yet shines. Even at night time, the sun is yet shining and the moon is reflecting its light. So, when it looks like it is setting, it isn't.

Clear and Sunny – Many days are clear and sunny, and we want them to last forever. Unfortunately, they are not always that way. But, enjoy them while they are and remember them when it's not so clear and sunny. They are times of rest and refreshing.

Humid – hot and sticky, muggy. When life gets hot and sticky, remember how Adam heard the voice of God walking in the cool of the day. Get in that hidden (cool) restful place in God and stay cool.

Overcast – Some days look dreary and if we're not careful, we will allow the way things look to cause dreariness in our lives. We will have overcast days but the sun is still shining. It just chooses to stay hidden behind the clouds sometimes. Don't let that order your day.

Mild Day – Thank God for the Spring, uh? We truly welcome the mildness of times when we've been through the blizzards of winter. It's not cold and it's not hot – it's just right; just like baby bear's chair, bed, and soup in the story of the three bears.

Winds – Light and Variable/Breezy or Gusty? I bet I can answer for most of us. We would prefer light and variable or breezy, to gusty. Some times those wind gusts can be real strong and cause us to be carried about where we don't particularly want to go. Make sure you have your armor on so you can stay grounded.

Windy/Chilly - Now, there is nothing worst than the cold than when there's strong winds accompanying it causing the chill factor.

Cloudy/Partly Cloudy/Increasing Cloudiness – Some time clouds gather and it looks like rain, but the rain never comes. The way we perceive things are not always the way they truly are. We must walk by faith and not by sight.

Cloudy All Day – Some time circumstances, situations and conditions exist in our lives lasting momentarily, all day, all night, all week, all month, all year and for several years, but the clouds always move away. They are temporary.

Chance of Rain – Be prepared just in case. Take your rain gear (umbrella, coat, boots).
Keep your armor on.

Showers – Light – You welcome the sprinkling on your face when there are light showers. It feels fun and refreshing. Even the sun is still shining and some time there are rainbows in the sky.

Rain All Day – Wet weather; scattered showers; mixed clouds. When we were small children, we hated for it to rain, especially all day. We wanted to go outside to play. I think the rain outside helps to keep us inside at times. We might think twice before going outside. Take the time to rest.

Rain All Week – Don't complain. Father is watering the scenery, providing for the thirsty, and cleansing the atmosphere.

No Rain – Some time days, weeks, and even months go by when there is no rain. Some might say, "This is good." But we need the rain in more ways than one. We can enjoy those dry days, but we must welcome the wet ones also. Now if we had only dry days, there would be no growth, no cleansing, no refreshing, no quenching for our thirst.

Flooding – Stuff happens. However overwhelming, stay afloat. Sometimes life comes at you so fast you don't know what hit you and from whence it came. The flood does subside. There are different purposes for floods, some destroy while others remove and cleanse.

Cold – Ever lived in an area where the weather was cold most of the time? A few days of sunshine and high temperatures had to be marvelous for you. In our lives, there are seasons that are "cold" for a long period of time. What to do then? Stay inside if possible and dress warm if you must go out.
There is a secret place in the Most High set up especially for times like these.

Dry/Fair/Unseasonably Cold – Sometimes the weather is just cold. There is no snow, no ice, no wind – just coldness.

Freezing – When the weather forecasters predict a freeze, they normally advise us to leave our spigots dripping so our pipes won't freeze up and burst. Wrap up, for the freeze is just temporary. Enjoy the warmth on the inside.

Below Freezing – Just when you think it can't get any worst, things seem to go under; below the surface – below freezing. Throw on another log, turn up the heat, and rest for a while. You now have a chance to do some of the things that you've been planning to do on the "inside" that you never got to do when the weather was nice.

Snow Flurries – Most of us welcome snow flurries because they are short lived. These are the times you keep an eye on the flurries to see if they continue and stick or if they stop. Prepare accordingly.

Inches of Snow - The problem comes when the snow continues for days and weeks at a time building up walls around us, making travel difficult (on foot or in driving).

Heavy snow and rain – Now, the snow and rain is not so bad together. Slushy and messy, but okay; no freezing rain welcome.

Rain mixed with ice – Sleet – Now, here is a problem. Don't make too many plans where you have to walk or drive. Cuddle up with the family.

Icy – Sheets of ice – not good. Sometimes the ice is referred to as "black ice" because you can't see it. You only see and feel the results of it when you begin to slide on top of it. Some time you have to go slow just in case the ice is buried beneath the snow or is blended in with the color of the road.

Severe Thunder Storms
The lightning comes and causes the thunder. When I was young, thunder and lightning devastated me. You didn't have to tell me more than once to be quiet or to be still. I just knew that if I was uncovered and out in the weather, I would be struck and killed by the lightning. Some of our trials are just like that. We seem to be bombarded from every side. We try to hide. And soon the storm is over. The rain stops, the clouds move away, and the sun shines through again.

Thunder Storms – Damaging winds. These thunderstorms are milder than the previous ones. Because we've matured – going through many, yet you survived. Still here, and still going on. So, the storms still arise, but you just take this time to be still and know….

There are some days that's just noisy and flashy. It's thundering and lightening in our lives and we can't wait for the storm to pass over. Know that is will!

Tornadoes – Tornadoes have a tremendous amount of power and some times move you completely out of your place to another place in an instant. Hurricanes can also produce tornadoes that add to the storm's destructive power. Tornadoes tend to occur mainly during day time hours. When the warning comes, you just move to that small interior room, away from the windows.

Hurricanes – Ingredients include pre-existing disturbances. If the right conditions persist long enough, they can combine to produce violent winds, incredible waves, torrential rains, and floods.

Cyclones – Classified in three categories: Tropical Depression –
Winds of 38 mph
Tropical Storm
Winds of 39-73 mph
Hurricane – Winds of 74 mph or higher

Lower category storms can sometimes inflict greater damage (and loss of life) than higher ones depending on where they strike and the particular hazards they bring. Flooding is its main thing.

Sand Storms – When I was in Saudi, I experienced my first sand storm. They are the same as rain storms, but its sand instead of rain. You get sand in your eyes, mouth, hair, and on your clothing. When you're driving, you have to use your windshield wipers just as you do when it's raining. No matter what kind of storms – rain or sand or snow – they do past.

Adverse Weather Conditions – We will experience adverse conditions at any given moment. It looked as though it was a calm clear day, but things turned abruptly for the worst. You thought you were quite prepared for the weather but it changed on you. LAUGH!

Fog/Smog – Poor visibility. On these days, no matter how you're traveling (walking and/or driving), precaution is advised.

Large Hail – If you're like me, you wonder where does the large balls come from all of a sudden, hitting so hard so as to dent, break, and destroy things. They damage property and people. You definitely want to find a place to enter. You don't want a headache, do you? That's how situations, circumstances, and conditions appear in our lives at times…enormous and sudden.

Mud Slides – It's amazing how much mud can slide at once. Without warning, things are moved out of their place. Sounds like weak foundations. Something must have happened to change what was underneath or maybe whatever was built, the architect did not make sure of a solid foundation.

DIFFERENT SEASONS BRING ABOUT DIFFERENT WEATHER PATTERNS.

Fall

Summer

Winter

Spring

WEATHER GEAR

Don't plan your day around the weather; plan the weather around your day.
Dress accordingly.

Check your local forecast
Check your extended forecast
Check your local conditions
Check your tides – low or high
Check your barometric pressure
Check your 7-day outlook
Consider your outdoor activities

BE PREPARED

Put on the whole armor of God that you may be able to stand against the wiles of the devil, and having done all to stand, stand.

Helmet of Salvation
Breastplate of Righteousness
Feet shod with Peace
Sword of the Spirit
Shield of Faith
Praying always.

Now you are a thermostat that others can set their days by.

THORNS AMONG ROSES

THORN: WHAT'S A THORN?

A thorn is a sharp excrescence on a plant, a sharp pointed abortive branch; a prickle that causes sharp pain, irritation, or discomfort. In one's life, a thorn is used to describe a nuisance, a bother, torture, a plague, a curse, a pest, torment, a hassle, an affliction, a scourge, a chronic infirmity, an annoyance or trouble.

Matthew 13:7 speaks about the thorn in the parable of the sowing of seeds.... "And some fell among thorns; and the thorns sprung up and choked them." **Matthew 13:22**.... "He also that received seed among the thorns is he that hears the word; and the care of this world, the deceitfulness of riches, and the lust of other things entering in choke the word and he becomes unfruitful." **Mark 4:7, 18** says it this way.... "And some fell among thorns, and the thorns grew up, and choked it (the Word), and it yielded no fruit."

Don't allow the thorns of life to separate you from your creator and maker. They are present, along with the flower, but they (for the most part) can be avoided with careful handling, and can be removed. **What is your Thorn? What's choking you?**

Let's look at another side of the thorn:

.... And lest I should be exalted above measure through the abundance of the revelations, there was given to me a thorn in the flesh, the messenger of Satan to buffet me, lest I should be exalted above measure. (2 Corinthians 12:7)
.... Therefore, I take pleasure in infirmities, in reproaches, in necessities, in persecutions, in distresses for Christ's sake, for when I am weak, then am I strong. (2 Corinthians 12:10)

Didn't think a thorn could be a blessing, did you? Being made uncomfortable is not always a bad thing. It could be for your good and God's glory. **What is there among you that seems difficult but benefits you?**

ROSE: WHAT'S A ROSE?

A rose is a petal flower that's arrayed in different colors. The rose is something to behold, no matter what color it may be. In spite of all the thorns that leads up to the rose, nothing can compare to its beauty. Remember that the bush does not just consist of the sticky thorns, but bursts forth into a sweet and beautiful flower. The pain that you feel from the thorn lasts but for a moment.

Remember, the day does not bring forth only rain, but sunshine also; even sometimes during the rain the sunshine bursts forth. Don't get stuck by the thorn – cut it off or wear a glove, and by all means pick the rose.

There is a Rose for each thorn that sticks you

THORN: Adultery

ROSE: Adultery is unfaithfulness in the worst form. As in the natural, also in the spirit. Have you been unfaithful to your spouse? Have you been unfaithful to God? Oh, you didn't know that we commit adultery against the Lord? Are you in a contract or a covenant?

THORN: An Abomination

ROSE: The Lord have given us those things that are abominable to Him. We must steer clear of them. We don't want to be on God's bad side. He is love, but He is also a jealous God, a consuming fire, and expects a better response to His loving kindness.

THORN: Aloneness

ROSE: It is a good thing to be alone sometimes. Most of us can actually hear from God better when we're alone with Him. Our Father is always speaking so we can always hear Him whether alone or in a crowd. In our alone time with Him, we can truly enjoy the simple splendor and awesomeness of the glory of God in everything. It is equally good to be around others in relationship.

THORN: An Abortion, Miscarriage, Barrenness

ROSE: All of these hindrances come into our lives at some time. They don't only refer to unborn babies and unborn dreams, visions, books, gifts, talents, etc. They happen by our doing and by unavoidable or uncontrolled circumstances. Declare God's word concerning these and seek His face concerning your particular situation. God is all about fruitfulness and multiplication. On the other hand, if you've allowed something to be conceived in your womb (your life) that is out of God's will for you, by all means ABORT. Be barren to the things of the enemy.

THORN: A Bad Habit

ROSE: Heard of opposites? Turn a bad habit into a good one. Just because you are at a certain place, does not mean that you have to stay in that place. Line yourself up with the Word of God, then start making good habits.

THORN: Bitterness

ROSE: Bitter or Better? We have a choice. In our lives, we are afforded many opportunities to be bitter – because situations, conditions, and circumstances will tell you that you are justified in becoming bitter, but not so. You can choose to take those lemons and make lemonade. We are to learn from others' mistakes and ours. So, release the bitterness. It too, comes along with other negative spirits.

THORN: A Broken Dream

ROSE: So, you saw yourself in a place, with a person, on a job, with a business, but you haven't seen it materialize. Don't give up on your dream – keep dreaming. Be mindful not to do too much dreaming and miss the manifestation of it. As long as the dream lines up with God's will, it will come to pass.

THORN: Blurred Vision

ROSE: So you're not seeing clearly. Invest in a pair of spiritual eye glasses. Pray to the Father and ask Him to help you to see through His eyes; only then can you see clearly. Read and study and hear His words – your eyesight will change.

THORN: Chastisement

ROSE: ...is not punishment. It is meant for correction. The creator chastens those He loves. Because of it, we should become better (not bitter). Welcome the correction; don't push it away. Learn from I so you can chastise those you love....your child/children.

THORN: A Clique You Want To Fit In With

ROSE: I heard my pastor say "Don't make anyone a priority in your life who has made you an option in theirs." I agree wholeheartedly. Don't try to fit in. You won't fit. Allow God to send you those who are connected to your destiny. Everyone does not fit that mold. And it doesn't matter whether it's family or not. The enemy will send some – they will not celebrate you but will try to destroy you. If God removes someone from your life, release them. Ask Him to help you recognize those that He sends.

THORN: Complaining/Murmuring

ROSE: Remember the children of Israel after they left Egypt...they murmured and complained and it displeased God. Only two of the thousands entered the promised land. If we trust God, then we'll wait patiently on Him, knowing that He keeps His promises, cannot lie, and watches over His Word to perform it. We ought to know that all things work together for good to them that love God and that are called according to His purpose.

THORN: Coveting

ROSE: You don't have to want what belongs to someone else. God have what you need already booked for you. No one else can have what HE has for you. Rejoice with and for others in their blessings for yours is not the same as theirs.

THORN: A Curse

ROSE: God does curse but He does not curse His children. There are curses that come about by the hand or mouth of others (and sometimes we pronounce curses on ourselves in ignorance). We can bring about curses in our lives by disobeying the Word of God. Obedience brings us back into the blessings of God. This is a wide subject. If you are convinced that you are experiencing such, please get help from your pastor.

THORN: A Death

ROSE: So someone close to you died. Why are you angry? I can understand being saddened because you'll miss them, but why are you angry? Did you give them life? What did you do for them while they were alive? Anyone that dies in the Lord is eternally blessed. If you stepped off the scene right now, will you see them again?
Well, we're all headed that way – death, I mean. It's up to us to decide what dimension we will enter afterwards

THORN: Debt

ROSE: Search out the reason why you have the debt. Pay it off – resolve the issue surrounding it. Owe no man anything – only love.

THORN: Defeat

ROSE: In Him, there is no defeat. If you are in Him and He is in you, there is no defeat. That belongs to Hell, not you.

THORN: Disability

ROSE: God has given us ability – disability is not His plan for us. Someone who is physically challenged can be assigned in that place for the glory of God. Remember the young man in the Bible who was born blind? The disciples inquired of the Lord asking who had sinned that this one was born that way. Jesus told them that no one had sinned, but for the glory of God was he born blind. Sometimes, I think God wants to see how are we responding to these so-called "disabled" people. Are we going to love them as we do those who are not disabled? Are we going to help them? Are we going to snub our nose at them as if we are better somehow? We don't have all the answers to the question "WHY" but God is able to do exceeding and abundantly above anything we can ask or think according to the power that works in us – He is that power in us – we must work it.

THORN: Discouragement

ROSE: Are you discouraged? God instructed Joshua to be encouraged in Him and in the power of His might. In God is our courage for we know that we are not alone and that the one who is in us, with us, and for us is The Mighty One. We have no reason to be discouraged when we truly trust in Him with all our hearts and not lean to our own understanding. If you are discouraged today, take the **Dis-** and the **-ment** off and stand in **courage**.

THORN: Disappointment

ROSE: Are you disappointed? God has an appointment set just for us. There are times I've felt like I would never enter the examining room because of the time. God assures me that my time is not His time. He is never late and never wrong. Waiting is one of our "testing" tools. The Word says for us to allow patience to do her thing so that we won't lack anything. We can't get weary in well doing, but we can be faithful in doing well until our time comes.

THORN: Disagreement

ROSE: Is there some disagreement between you and your spouse, you and your friend, you and your neighbor, you and your child/children? Can you agree to disagree and still move on? Remember love and forgiveness is the key. Work to change what you can but you can't change others. Accept what you can't change and work around them, take authority where your child/children are concerned but don't disregard their stand altogether because God uses them too. Let love and the Word of God be the foundation and basis for coming into agreement.

THORN: Disobedience

ROSE: Is it possible that you possess a disobedient spirit? Run from it. Denounce it. Rebuke it. Get rid of it? How, you may say. BE OBEDIENT!

THORN: Failure

ROSE: Have you experienced failure in some area or areas of your life? Or does it look like, feel like, sound like FAILURE? Well, in Christ there is no failure. That thought or idea did not come from God. Cast that down and bring it into captivity for it exalts itself against the knowledge of God. If you need to begin again, do it. If you need to stop what you're doing, stop it. If you need to do something different, dig in; but do not accept failure. It does not belong to you. You are already a winner.

THORN: A Family Member

ROSE: Is someone in your family causing you problems? Address the problem, then take action to do whatever you can to erase or correct it. If you can't do anything, then cast it upon the Lord for He cares for you.

THORN: Fear

ROSE: The One who created us did not make us with a spirit of fear but made us up with a spirit of love, power, and a sound mind. Our only fear should be a reverence respect for the Creator. FEAR is false evidence appearing real, set up by the enemy of us all. Get rid of all demonic paraphernalia in your life – television shows, movies, books, games, activities, etc. And, don't allow fear to overtake you being anxious over some- thing that IS not or MAY be.

THORN: A Financial Struggle

ROSE: I've had one for years. So, what are you going to do about it? Maybe you're the reason why you're struggling and maybe you're not? What can you do to change it? Maybe someone else caused you to be in a certain place financially that you normally wouldn't be. Do what you can do to change it and TRUST GOD. We can be expecting, but not preparing for opportunities to get into order.

THORN: Forsaken

ROSE: Do you feel forsaken? The Lord has promised never to leave us nor forsake us, so you just put that thought from the enemy right out of your mind. God is big and bad enough to carry out anything that He has promised. He cannot lie. He said it and it is so.
Consider yourself "unforsaken."

Victoria R. Bradley

THORN: A Gossiping Tongue

ROSE: Have trouble keeping the pink tornado from tearing up stuff? Start from your heart, hide the Word in it, then let it roll off your tongue. Choose not to continue in it. Don't take any garbage in and you won't have any to dump out.

THORN: Hatred

ROSE: Where does that come from? The only thing we should hate is SIN. There should never be a hatred pointed toward a person. We may hate something that a person does or does not do, but we should not hate the person. We have power enough in us to love the person and speak to the thing what God has said about it.

THORN: Idolatry

ROSE: God says, "I am a jealous God. You shall have no other God before me." No other person, No thing, Not yourself – none of these should be worshipped – only Father God. The little gods will not do – He is the only true and living God! Worship HIM.

THORN: Ignorance

ROSE: The Lord winked at ignorance once, but not anymore. We are all able to grow up in Christ. Facts are everywhere but Truth has to be desired. It is there, but do we recognize it? Every day you wake up, the opportunity is there to learn. Knowledge is power. The Word tells us that we perish because of the lack of. Pray, Read, Study, Listen, Invest in yourself. Ignorance is a choice also.

THORN: Imagined Nations

ROSE: Cast them all down.

THORN: A Learning Disability

ROSE: Are you having problems with learning in a particular area? Seek God about it and hear what He says about the matter. Do you need to know that particular thing to complete your destiny? Or is it just something you want to do to satisfy your flesh, or to satisfy a person? There are more ways than one to learn. Search it out.

THORN: A Lie told to you or about you

ROSE: Remember, Satan is the father of lies and anyone who he fathers can do nothing different. Liars are here because he is here, but the truth always prevail. Rest in knowing the truth and in knowing that our Creator knows it too. The ones being used by the enemy has to reap what they sow. It's the Word.

THORN: Limits Placed On You By Yourself and Others

ROSE: When our perception is small and when it is not aligned with the Creator's, and when we measure ourselves by others, what others say and do, we tend to judge our place right there. Instead, we need to agree with what the manufacturer says about us and proceed into our destiny. God is not limited. He is out of the box. That's where we should be – out of the box. How big is your God?

THORN: Loneliness

ROSE: Loneliness and boredom are cousins. A state of mind, I think. Many people are lonely in a crowd and bored with thousands of opportunities all around. You can choose to be or not. Learn to seize every opportunity to interact with your environment, whether with the creator, another person (you don't have to know them), nature (so much glory), things (oh too many to mention). Don't sit around idling – there's always something to do-just open your eyes and your mind. There are things on the inside of you and on the outside of you. Engage.

THORN: A Lost Loved One

ROSE: Do you have a loved one that's lost? Well, he or she is not lost to God. He knows exactly where they are. He knows exactly where we are...even when we don't know where we are ourselves but think that we do. Place them in the Lord's hand and watch God reveal himself. God doesn't lose anything!

THORN: Loving One Who Does Not Love You

ROSE: Nowhere in the Word does it tell us that those we love will respond in love to us. It just tells us to love – God, our family, our friends, our enemies – there's no one left not to love. As long as you love, you are subject to be hurt. The flesh will hurt because it's not dead yet. Don't stop loving, just readjust your expectations and change your actions.

THORN: A Lust

ROSE: Do you have an unsatisfiable desire for something or someone? Is your desire for it more than your desire for the Lord? Is your flesh gratified by it? What does it add to you as a whole? Let LOVE replace it.

THORN: A Lying Tongue

ROSE: The Word tells us that liars have no place in the Kingdom of God, but they do have a place in the lake of fire. Allow the Holy Spirit to tame your tongue. First, by the heart, then what the mouth speaks.

THORN: Misplaced Emotions

ROSE: Do you have misplaced emotions? Are you making someone in your life a PRIORITY who in turn treats you as an option? Did someone do something for you that was their reasonable service any way but you've embraced it as something more? Do you feel obligated because of it or are they causing you to feel obligated because of it? You could become entangled in some relationships because of this. Watch and Pray.

THORN: A Misunderstanding

ROSE: So you've been misunderstood. You probably will be again. Or maybe you're the one that has misunderstood. It happens. Be led by the Spirit and do what He says to do about it. Sometimes you may be directed to a person to apologize or to explain and sometimes you may be directed to stand on the truth whereby you have been standing and do nothing. Knowing the truth will keep you free.

THORN: A Missing Limb

ROSE: You are an amputee. Your leg, arm, finger, toe, hip, etc. have been removed. That is not a reason to throw in the towel. It might be difficult or challenging but use it for good rather than for evil. Your physical limb may be missing but your spiritual limb is still intact. From what I understand (not an amputee), some things may be removed from us that other things may be grafted in.

THORN: A Need

ROSE: But my God shall supply all your need according to His riches in Glory by Christ Jesus. Only God knows what you need anyway.

THORN: A Negative Report

ROSE: The Word asks us "Whose report will you receive (believe)." Did you receive a negative report? The first thing you must ask yourself is: Who gave the report? Where did it come from? Then, answer your report. How do you answer? With the Word of God. Whatever God says about the situation, that is the only report that you must receive. Resist the <u>F</u>alse <u>E</u>vidence <u>A</u>ppearing <u>R</u>eal.

THORN: An Open Sore

ROSE: Have you allowed a past incident into your present? Is there an irritation in your spirit when you see someone who has hurt you in the past? Forgive and release. If you continue to allow that sore, it could turn to a cancer – in your spirit, your soul, and/or your body.

THORN: A Past Hurt

ROSE: Has something taken place in your past that you still are carrying around with you? Now, it is past so why are you still holding on to it? Can you go back and erase it or change it? No. So why not let it go? It has to be heavy – dead things are. What looked like a hurt could truly have been a blessing.

THORN: A Person, Place, or Thing

ROSE: Is there a person that has become a thorn in your flesh? In your spirit? Cut it off. If it offends you and cause you to go astray from the right way, get rid of him, her or it – whatever or whoever it may be. I heard my Pastor say that whatever does not ignite praise in you, it does not belong with you. I agree. Your loved one can be a thorn, so can your neighbor. If your day or week is messed up because of a person, place, or thing, they have too much control over you.

THORN: A Place

ROSE: Maybe your thorn is a place that you love or a place that you hate. What has the Father said about the place? Have you asked Him? Maybe the place is new to you and might be uncomfortable but it could indeed be the place where God wants you to be. It could be a temporary place or a permanent place. It could just be a 'testing' place. You may be uncomfortable in that place because you are used to an old place that you had to leave. God may be directing you to a new place. You may want to leave a place because others are leaving, but you are to remain. Seek the Lord.

THORN: Poverty/Lack

ROSE: A spirit from Hell, not one from Heaven. Does not belong to a child of God. Align yourself with the Word of God if you are not aligned.

THORN: Pride

ROSE: Pride comes before a fall. What is it that you have that was not given unto you? Everything you are or have, God has given it. So why act as though you originated anything? All that is good and right in or about you is the Lord. Without Him we are nothing. Don't put yourself or anyone or anything else on the throne of your heart – if you do, you can become lifted up in what got Satan kicked out of heaven.

THORN: Racism

ROSE: We were created and made by God and we had no choice in the matter. None of us is better or worse than the other. We are spirits that came from God, we have a soul, and live in a body (which is dirt). One pile of dirt is no better than another pile of dirt. Racism comes from hell. It is sin and there is no other way to put it. If you are guilty of it (especially if you call yourself a child of God), REPENT!

THORN: A Rape or Molestation

ROSE: As bad as it sounds, seems, or may have happened to you, you are still obligated to forgive. It could have been reversed. You could have been the one committing the act. Only by God's grace and mercy you are not the rapist or molester. The enemy wants to destroy you with the experience of the act, but you are better than the act itself.

THORN: A Reading Problem

ROSE: Is there an illiterate problem in your life? Were you robbed of an education at an early age? Well, it's not too late to learn now. We are in school all of our lives, so why not continue from where you left of? There is help all around you. Begin from where you are.

THORN: Rebellion

ROSE: Somewhere in the Word, it says that it's hard to kick against the prick. You can't kick against God. He is our creator and maker. He IS the potter and we are the clay in His hands. If its sin you're coming up against, that's good, but if its righteousness you're coming up against, you can't win. You're just going around and around the mountain, bringing condemnation upon yourself.

THORN: Rejection

ROSE: Rejection is never an easy thing but remember they rejected Christ, but He is still Christ. Look at who's rejecting you. If it's not Christ, you have nothing to worry about. People who may be judging you and choosing to leave you out of their circle are not worthy of your presence. Then, looking at it from another angle, it may not be a rejection at all, it might just be the Lord keeping you from wrong company.

THORN: A Relationship Gone Sour

ROSE: It takes two to form a relationship. If you are the only one giving or the only one taking, there is no relationship there. Your first relationship should be that fellow-ship with the one who made you. All "so called" relationships are not forever. Some people are to be in our lives for a season, and some are to be there all of our lives. Your parents, spouse and children are mostly likely to be there in relationship. Those with whom you are in relation with should bring something to your life. Don't stay in any relationship where you are bound (unproductive).

THORN: Selfishness

ROSE: Love is not selfish, but love is kind. Loving yourself more than you should makes you selfish. Loving others as you love yourself makes you selfless. There is enough room to love you and others. Even more above that is the fact that you should love the Lord with all your heart first. Love is the foundation for selflessness.

THORN: Sickness, Disease

ROSE: Sickness and Disease does not come from the Lord. The Lord went about healing all forms of sickness and disease. Now, sin opens the door for many things; sickness and disease are two of them. We, as the children of God, were healed by Jesus' stripes, so we don't have to receive these in ourselves. Yes, our bodies come under attacks but we cause many of these attacks – our eating habits, our speaking, our misuse of our bodies, our thinking, and so on. Some afflictions are allowed for God's glory, but sickness and disease does not belong to us. MEDITATE

THORN: A Situation, Condition, Circumstance

ROSE: These are where the facts lie; the truth is what God says!

THORN: Slothfulness

ROSE: Does the spirit of slothfulness hang over you? Are you slack and/or mediocre in your dealings? Denounce that spirit and step up

THORN: Something Stolen

ROSE: When someone steals something of yours, it's very painful; especially if it's someone you trusted that did the stealing. You are still responsible to forgive them.
That is your RESPONSE as a child of the King. Don't worship anything so much that you can't forgive someone if that thing is missing from your life.

THORN: Sorrow/Grief

ROSE: Sorrow and Grief are spirits. As the preacher says, "There is a time for everything under the sun." There is a temporary place for sorrow and grief. It is not to take up residence inside of you. Whatever happens to you is common to man, but God has provided a way of escape for each of us – He won't allow us to be tempted above that which we are able to bear.

THORN: A Spoken Word

ROSE: There may be words spoken to you, about you, around you, for you. Take only what your spirit receives from God. Discard the rest.

THORN: Stealing

ROSE: Why would you want to take something that is not yours? Why would you want something that God did not give to you? I have often heard that a liar will also steal. Well, it is so. If you are a liar, you can tell yourself that that thing that you want is yours, when the truth is that it is not. So, as you believe your lie, you will act on it. Work for what you want. Ask, and seek God for what he has for you. He has more than enough to go around.

THORN: Strife

ROSE: Strife should have no place in your life. You have no room for it. Whatever is causing your strife, you need to erase it. Deal with it. Forsake it. Remove it. Strife brings other spirits with it, so get rid of it – quickly.

THORN: A Stronghold

ROSE: Is there someone or something that is orchestrating your life other than your creator and maker? That is a stronghold that needs to be weakened and released. Don't give a person or a thing that much power over you. If it's pushing you toward your destiny, it's good. If it's pulling you away from your journey, it's not good. Take time to recognize any and all strongholds in your life and dismiss them.

THORN: A Struggle Within, With Self, Flesh

ROSE: Struggling? Struggle is not always bad. Some time we must struggle to get out of a net, a jam, a mess, a group, etc. if that's what it takes to get free. But when we take the time to listen to wisdom, most times struggle is not an issue. Struggling to be free and not in bondage is good. Struggling to stay in bondage when there is present help to become free is not good.

THORN: A Studder in Speech

ROSE: Are you in a box because of a speech impediment? God can deliver you from it. It's nothing impossible for Him. Only believe. It is conquerable. Submit your instrument to Him, the one who made it.

THORN: Success

ROSE: Have you become successful in what you've been after? Watch your steps up and don't step on anyone. Remember that true success is in the true riches of God, which resides on the inside of you. Money, Stuff, Things, People, Power does not necessarily spell success. These things without God spell nothing. If God is not the head of and is not being glorified in whatever it is that you feel is success, it is not.

THORN: A Temptation

ROSE: Every one of us have them. The thing is, we should not yield to them. Having them present themselves in our lives is common, but yielding to them is sin. The Word says that there is no temptation that is not common to men, but God has already provided a way of escape that we may be able to overcome them. It's only a test.

THORN: Unforgiveness

ROSE: Within the Lord's prayer, we are instructed to forgive if we wish to be forgiven. Another place in scripture tells us to forgive our brothers seventy times for the same thing. We are all capable of and do commit the same sins – maybe in smaller or larger degrees, maybe in different degrees, but whatever the degree, we are all guilty of sin and need the Father's forgiveness. So why not forgive one another. We can't move forward unless we do.

THORN: Ungratefulness

ROSE: Being honest, are you an ungrateful person? Do you feel that everybody and the world owes you something? They don't. And guess what? It's not about you, it's about Jesus. The Word says we are to be thankful in everything. His grace, mercy, and His awesome love….

THORN: An Uncertainty

ROSE: Seek God and do nothing until He instructs you to.

THORN: What People Say

ROSE: What people say does not matter. What God says matters more.

THORN: What People Think

ROSE: What people think does not matter. What God thinks matters more.

THORN: What You Don't Say

ROSE: Are you in agreement with it? Whatever the case. We should be bold to speak to our circumstances, situations, and conditions. If injustice is happening, are you speaking up against it or are you keeping silent? If justice is happening, are you speaking up in agreement with it?

THORN: What You Say

ROSE: The power of life and death is in our tongue. We are what we say. Where we are today is a result of what we have been saying. What we say are seeds. We sow them, so what we sow will grow – either good or bad.

THORN: Wickedness

ROSE: Why sit around thinking up evil things to do unto another? You will never stand
before God in wickedness. Instead of idleness where the devil can work in you, why not get busy in God's work. The results are marvelous.

THORN: Worry

ROSE: Do you pray? Then, why worry? If you are going to worry instead of believing in what you pray and in the one to whom you pray, don't pray. If you are praying according to God's will, you have no need to worry. You have blessed assurance.

THORN: Wrong Done To You

ROSE: If someone has wronged you, get over it. Forgive them and move on. You don't have to live with them and now you know just how to deal with them. They may just be at a different level than you are. Pray for them, love them, and watch God work. I didn't say that it would be easy, but make the step. People grow, people change, things change. Don't forget that.

THORN: A Wrongful Death

ROSE: So, you feel that the death of your loved one was wrong. Was the death of Jesus wrong? God never promised us eternal life on the earth and He never asked our opinion of how we would leave the earth. Our expiration date is in His hands, not ours.

THORN: Your Mind/Your Thinking

ROSE: The Bible tells us to renew our mind with the Word and think on things that are
pure. Our minds are the battlefield where warfare takes place. We need to keep our minds loaded with the Word that always defeats our enemy.

SMELL THE ROSES

Remember:

No temptation has seized you except what is common to man. And God is faithful; he will not let you be tempted beyond what you can bear. But when you are tempted, he will also provide a way out so that you can stand up under it. 1 Corinthians 10:13

We fix our eyes not on what is seen, but on what is unseen. For what is seen is temporary, but what is unseen is eternal. 2 Corinthians 4:18

And we know that in all things God works for the good of those who love him, who have been called according to his purpose. Romans 8:28

For physical training is of some value, but godliness has value for all things, holding promise for both the present life and the life to come. 1 Timothy 4:8

A righteous man may have many troubles, but the Lord delivers him from them all. Psalm 34:19

Forgive us our debts, as we also have forgiven our debtors. Matthew 6:12

No weapon forged against you will prevail, and you will refute every tongue that accuses you. This is the heritage of the servants of the Lord, and this is their vindication from me, declares the Lord. Isaiah 54:17

The Lord has delivered us from all unrighteousness

I have given you authority to trample on snakes and scorpions and to overcome all the power of the enemy; nothing will harm you. Luke 10:19

Jesus answered, "It is written: Man does not live on bread alone. Luke 4:4

The Spirit of the Lord is on me, because he has anointed me to preach good news to the poor. He has sent me to proclaim freedom for the prisoners and recovery of sight for the blind, to release the oppressed, to proclaim the year of the Lord's favor. Luke 4:18-19

> We are Kings and Priest in the Earth
> We are Christ in the Earth
> We are Salt of the Earth
> We are the Light of the World
> 			Matthew 5:13-14 and Revelations 1:6

We are Seated Together in heavenly places in Christ Jesus...

We rest, rule, reign, subdue, take authority, dominate, legislate, veto, declare, decree

Trust in the Lord with all your heart and lean not on your own understanding; in all your ways acknowledge him, and he will make your paths straight. Proverbs 3:5-6

We are Not Our Own

The Victory is already ours

He has given His angels charge over us to keep us in all our ways.

Jesus ever lives to make intercession for us. Hebrews 7:25
For thou has delivered my soul from death, mine eyes from tears, and my feet from falling. I will walk before the Lord in the land of the living. Psalm 116:8-9

He restores my soul. He leads me in the paths of righteousness for His name's sake. He prepares a table before me in the presence of mine enemies. Psalm 23:3, 5

Restore unto me the joy of Thy salvation; and uphold me with Thy free spirit. Psalm 51:12

And I will restore to you the years that the locust has eaten, the cankerworm, and the caterpillar, and the palmerworm. My great army which I sent among you. Joel 2:25

And forgive us our debts, as we forgive our debtors. Matthew 6:12

Be kindly affectionate one to another with brotherly love, in honor preferring one another; not slothful in business; fervent in spirit; serving the Lord. Romans 12:10-11

And everyone that has forsaken houses, or brethren, or sisters, or father, or mother, or wife, or children, or lands, for My sake, shall receive an hundredfold and shall inherit everlasting life. Matthew 19:29

For a small moment have I forsaken you; but with great mercies will I gather you. Isaiah 54:7

For I will restore health unto you, and I will heal you of your wounds... Jeremiah 30:17

AVOID THE THORNS IF AT ALL POSSIBLE

You've seen in the previous pages of the book, some of the many thorns that grace the way all the way up to the beautiful rose. There are some we can avoid and others that we can't.

Thorns can be in many such forms:

Adultery
Anger
Backbiting
Bad Habits
Bitterness
Busyness
Carelessness
Covering Sin
Covetous
Curses
Debt
Deceit
Disobedience
Disagreement
Dishonesty
Distrust
Doubleminded
Emotional baggage
Envy
Failure
Fear
Gossiping
Hatred
Idolatry
Ignorance
Indecisiveness
Injustice
Jealousy

Laziness
Life
Loneliness
Lust
Lying
Murmuring and Complaining
Offense
Poor Perception
Pride
Procrastination
Rage
Rejection
Saying the Wrong Thing
Selfishness
Sickness
Shortcomings
Slothfulness
Sorrow and Grief
Stealing
Strife
Stuck on Stupid
Success
Unbelief
Unforgiveness
Unfriendly
Ungrateful
Unthankful
Wickedness
Wrong Information
Yielding to Temptation

But I say to you that whoever looks at a woman to lust for her has already committed adultery with her in his heart. Matt 5:28

For out of the heart proceed evil thoughts, murders, adulteries, fornications, thefts, false witness, blasphemies. These are the things which defile a man, Matt 15:19-20

Therefore, whatever you want men to do to you, do also to them, for this is the Law and the Prophets. Matt 7:12

...Do you not perceive that whatever enters a man from outside cannot defile him, because it does not enter his heart but his stomach, and is eliminated...What comes out of a man, that defiles a man. For from within, out of the heart of men, proceed evil thoughts, adulteries, fornications, murders, thefts, covetousness, wickedness, deceit, lewdness, an evil eye, blasphemy, pride, foolishness. All these evil things come from within and defile a man. Mark 7:18-23

And the Lord said to Samuel, Heed the voice of the people in all that they say to you; for they have not rejected you, but they have rejected Me, that I should not reign over them. 1 Sam 8:7

But you have today rejected your God, who Himself saved you from all your adversities and your tribulations; and you have said to Him, "No, set a king over us!" 1 Sam 10:19

For Rebellion is as the sin of witchcraft, and stubbornness is as iniquity and idolatry, because you have rejected the word of the Lord, He also has rejected you from being king. 1 Sam 15:23

Has a nation changed its gods; Which are not gods? But my people have changed their Glory for what does not profit. Be astonished, O heavens, at this and be horribly afraid; Be very desolate, says the Lord, for My people have committed two evils: they have forsaken Me, the fountain of living waters, and hewn themselves cisterns-broken cisterns that can hold no water.
Jere 2:11-13

Death and life are in the power of the tongue. And those who love it will eat its fruit. Prov 18:21

Little children, keep yourselves from idols. Amen! 1 John 5:21

Now the works of the flesh are evident, which are: adultery, fornication, uncleanness, lewdness, idolatry, sorcery, hatred, contentions, jealousies, outbursts of wrath, selfish ambitions, dissensions, heresies, envy murders, drunkenness, revelries, and the like; of which I tell you beforehand, just as I told you in time past, that those who practice such things will not inherit the kingdom of God. Gal 5:19-21

For if you forgive men their trespasses, your heavenly Father will also forgive you, but if you do not forgive men their trespasses, neither will your Father forgive your trespasses. Matt 6:14-15

Don't allow the thorns of life to separate you from your Creator and Maker, God. They are present along with the rose, but they (for the most part) can be avoided or removed; and if not, they might just be blessings from the Lord.

Victoria R. Bradley

I WANT TO BE A "COVER GIRL"

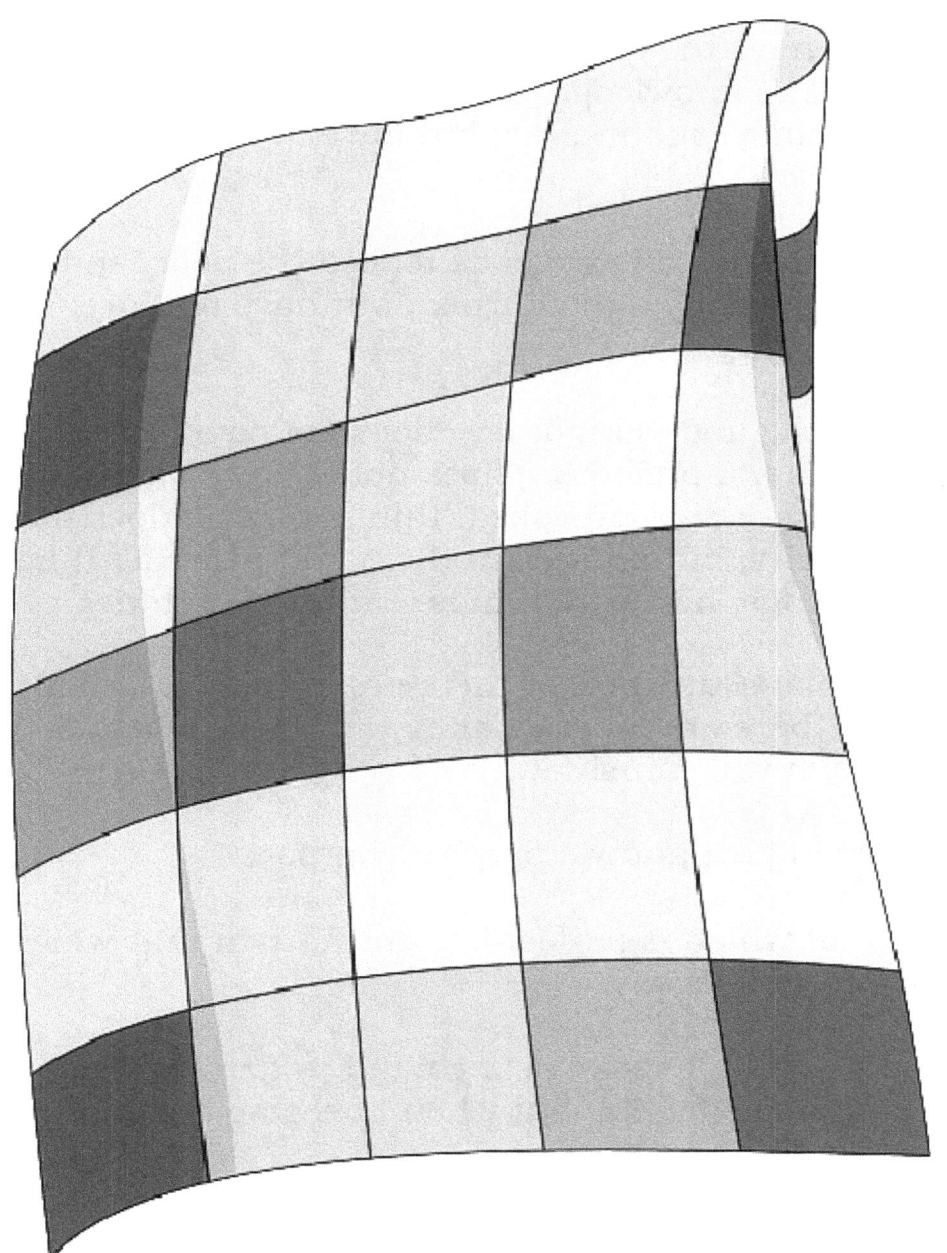

LOVE IS THE BLANKET THAT COVERS
Thou shalt love the Lord thy God with all thy heart, and with all thy soul, and with all thy mind...Thou shalt love thy neighbor as thyself.

Though I speak with the tongues of men and of angels, but have not love, I have become sounding brass or a clanging cymbal.

And though I have the gift of prophecy, and understand all mysteries and all knowledge, and though I have all faith, so that I could remove mountains, but have not love, I am nothing.

And though I bestow all my goods to feed the poor, and though I give my body to be burned, but have not love, it profits me nothing.

Love suffers long and is kind; love does not envy; love does not parade itself, is not puffed up; does not behave rudely, does not seek its own, is not provoked, thinks no evil; does not rejoice in iniquity, but rejoices in the truth; bears all things, believes all things, hopes all things, endures all things.

Love never fails. But whether there are prophecies, they will fail; whether there are tongues, they will cease; whether there is knowledge, it will vanish away.

For we know in part and we prophesy in part.

But when that which is perfect has come, then that which is in part will be done away.

When I was a child, I spoke as a child, I understood as a child, I thought as a child; but when I became a man, I put away childish things.

For now, we see in a mirror, dimly, but then face to face. Now I know in part, but then I shall know just as I also am known.

And now abide faith, hope, love, these three; but the greatest of these is LOVE.

1 Corinthians 13

I WANT TO BE A COVER GIRL

As I sat one day watching television, the "Cover Girl" make-up commercial came on. The Lord began to deal with me about becoming a real cover girl (not make-up). Then he gave me the title for this book "I want to be a Cover Girl!" He began to minister to me about me and asked me what did it mean to "cover."

I looked it up and saw that **_Cover_** means: To place something upon or over, so as to protect or conceal, to overlay or spread with something; to put a cover or covering on; to wrap or clothe; to invest with a great deal of something; to extend over; to spread over the surface of; to hide or screen from view or knowledge; to protect or shield from harm, loss, or danger; to compensate or make up for; to make provision for; to be responsible for guarding, defending; to purchase. He said, "if that is the case, why aren't you covering your fellowmen?"

God began to read my email. For so many years I had uncovered instead of covered. Let me explain. Murder occurs in many ways. There is physical murder, spiritual murder, verbal murder, mental murder. Because I was a gossiper and a backbiter, sowing discord, murmuring and complaining, and judging - I was uncovering. True love was missing in my life. Yes, I loved but it was not from a pure heart…because love would not do those things. I was not only killing other people, but I was also killing myself and things in my life.

I used the instruments of teeth, tongue and voice for unrighteousness. We know that the power of life and death is in the tongue – in the words we say.

So, I started on a journey to change that bad habit, that sin, into good by changing my words. I had to study the word concerning love, pray and seek God so that my **heart and mind** would change, so that the words that came out of my mouth would change. Instead of speaking death, I now speak life.

Let's take a walk in the Word and look at some places where **covering** is emphasized.

I WANT TO BE A COVER GIRL

GOD COVERING WHAT WE CANNOT

Genesis 3:7, 21
The first lesson of covering is found in Genesis in reference to the Creator covering his creation, Adam and Eve (after they had disobeyed Him in the garden of Eden).

God had commanded Adam (and Eve) not to eat of one tree that was in the midst of the garden – the tree of the knowledge of good and evil. He informed them of the consequences of disobeying – death. Eve was deceived by the serpent, took and ate, and gave to Adam. Before they disobeyed, they were walking in abundant life (all good), had no knowledge of evil. They were naked and unashamed. After disobeying God, they became ashamed and afraid. They tried to **cover** themselves and hide themselves from the Lord God, which is utterly impossible. After their judgment, the Lord God made coats of skin for clothing for Adam and his wife.

Exodus 33:22-23
And it shall come to pass, while my glory passes by that I will put thee in a clift of the rock and will **cover** thee with my hand while I pass by, and I will take away mine hand and thou shall see my back parts, but my face shall not be seen.

Isaiah 51:16
And I have put my words in thy mouth and I have **covered** thee in the shadow of mine hand, that I may plant the heavens and lay the foundations of the earth and say unto Zion, Thou art my people.

Isaiah 61:10
I will greatly rejoice in the Lord; my soul shall be joyful in my God; for he has clothed me with the garments of salvation; he has **covered** me with the robe of righteousness…

I WANT TO BE A COVER GIRL

Ezekiel 37:6
And I will lay sinews upon you and will bring up flesh upon you, and **cover** you with skin, and put breath in you and you shall live and you shall know that I am the Lord.

Exodus 13:21-22 and 14:19-20/Psalm 105:39
Protective covering: When the children of Israel began their journey into the wilderness from Egypt, the Lord went before them by day in a pillar of cloud to lead the way and by night in a pillar of fire to give them light. This speaks to me about our **covering** – GOD, as He leads us and **covers** us. His presence is not only in us but is also with us.

Psalms 91:4/17:8/36:7/61:4/63:7/Ruth 2:12/Matthew 23:37
Providential protection and care: He who dwells in the secret place of the Most High shall abide under the shadow of the Almighty. He shall **cover** you with His feathers and under His wings you shall take refuge…Feathers and wings – definite coverings.

Habakkuk 3:3
God came from Teman and the Holy One from mount Paran. His glory **covered** the heavens and the earth was full of his praise.

GOD'S FORGIVENESS A COVERING

Psalm 32:1/Psalm 85:2/Romans 4:7
Thou has forgiven the iniquity of thy people; thou has **covered** all their sin.

Blessed are they whose iniquities/transgressions are forgiven and whose sins are **covered**.

I WANT TO BE A COVER GIRL

COVERING ONESELF IN HUMILITY

Jonah 3:8
But let man and beast be **covered** with sackcloth and cry mightily unto God: yea, let them turn everyone from his evil way, and from the violence that is in their hands.

Isaiah 37:1
And it came to pass when king Hezekiah heard it, that he rent his clothes and **covered** himself with sackcloth and went into the house of the Lord.

NAKEDNESS BEING COVERED

Genesis 9:20-23
Noah got drunk and was uncovered in his tent. His younger son saw his nakedness and went to his brothers. His brothers did not go in to the tent to look at his nakedness, but went in to the tent backwards with a **covering** to hide his nakedness. You know what that says to me? They could have gone into the tent and look upon their father's nakedness and made fun of it.
Nakedness speaks of Shame and Humiliation, contempt, our privacy; our transparency (Deuteronomy 27:16).

So, Shem and Japheth were a type of Christ. I believe the two of them represent Christ first as our mediator that **covers** us and second as we are Christ in the earth, we should **cover** each other.

I WANT TO BE A COVER GIRL

Exodus 20:26/28:42-43
Priestly **covering**: – "And you shall make for them linen trousers to cover their nakedness; they shall reach from the waist to the thighs….to hide the nakedness of priests." "Nor shall you go up by steps to My altar, that your nakedness may not be exposed on it." This being in contrast to heathen priests who often ministered in nakedness.

Ezekiel 16:8/Psalm 85:2
Now when I passed by thee, and looked upon thee, behold, thy time was the time of love: and I spread my skirt over thee and covered thy nakedness: yea, I swear unto thee and entered into a covenant with thee, saith the Lord God, and thou became mine. Israel played the harlot. Yet Thou hast forgiven the iniquity of thy people; thou hast **covered** all their sin.

Isaiah 57:8
Behind the doors also and the posts has thou set up thy remembrance: for thou has **discovered** thyself to another than me and art gone up; thou has enlarged thy bed and made thee a covenant with them; thou love their bed where thou saw it.

Hosea 2:9-10
Therefore, will I return and take away my corn in the time thereof and my wine in the season thereof and recover my wool and my flax given to **cover** her nakedness. And now will I **discover** her lewdness in the sight of her lovers and none shall deliver her out of mine hand.

Isaiah 47:3
Thy nakedness shall be **uncovered**, yea, thy shame shall be seen: I will take vengeance and I will not meet thee as a man.

I WANT TO BE A COVER GIRL

PEOPLE AS COVERING

Numbers 22:5-6
Speaks of us as covering: ...the people coming from Egypt (being so many) as to **cover** the face of the earth. They were feared as they multiplied and grew. The enemy wanted them cursed. This speaks to me about the Kingdom of God (us) covering the face of the earth – in authority (resting,

ruling and reigning), being fruitful and multiplying. There are those who fear us and wish to curse us, but Numbers records repeatedly, that what God blesses is blessed and no one can curse, and that which He curses is cursed, and no one can bless.

I WANT TO BE A COVER GIRL

ENEMIES OF GOD'S COVERING

Ezekiel 7:18
They shall also gird themselves with sackcloth and horror shall **cover** them; and shame shall be upon all faces, and baldness upon all their heads.

Micah 7:10
Then she that is mine enemy shall see it and shame shall **cover** her which said unto me, Where is the Lord they God? Mine eyes shall behold her; now shall she be trodden down as the mire of the streets.

Habakkuk 2:17
For the violence of Lebanon shall **cover** thee and the spoil of beasts which made them afraid because of men's blood and for the violence of the land, of the city and of all that dwell therein.

Psalm 44:15
My confusion is continually before me and the shame of my face has **covered** me.

Psalm 89:45
The days of his youth hast thou shortened: thou hast **covered** him with shame.

Isaiah 29:10
For the Lord has poured out upon you the spirit of deep sleep and has closed your eyes; the prophets and your rulers, the seers has he **covered**.

Psalm 71:13
Let them be confounded and consumed that are adversaries to my soul; let them be **covered** with reproach and dishonor that seek my hurt.

Psalm 109:29
Let mine adversaries be clothed with shame and let them **cover** themselves with their own confusion, as with a mantle.

Psalm 140:9
As for the head of those that compass me about, let the mischief of their own lips **cover** them.

Isaiah 60:2
For behold the darkness shall **cover** the earth and gross darkness the people, but the Lord shall arise upon thee and his glory shall be seen upon thee.

Isaiah 30:1
Woe to the rebellious children, saith the Lord, that take counsel but not of me; and that **cover** with a **covering**, but not of my spirit, that they may add sin to sin.

Ezekiel 32:7-8
And when I shall put thee out, I will cover the heaven and make the stars thereof dark; I will **cover** the sun with a cloud and the moon shall not give her light. All the bright lights of heaven will I make dark over thee, and set darkness upon thy land, saith the Lord God.

Matthew 10:26
Fear them not therefore for there is nothing **covered** that shall not be revealed; and hid, that shall not be known.

Isaiah 47:3
Thy nakedness shall be **uncovered**, yea, they shame shall be seen: I will take vengeance and I will not meet thee as a man.

Isaiah 22:17
Behold, the Lord will carry thee away with a mighty captivity and will surely **cover** thee. (seize)

Ezekiel 30:18
At Tehaphnehes also the day shall be darkened when I shall break there the yokes of Egypt: and the pomp of her strength shall cease in her; as for her, a cloud shall **cover** her and her daughters shall go into captivity.

Joshua 24:7
And when they cried unto the Lord, he put darkness between you and the Egyptians and brought the sea upon them, and **covered** them; and your eyes have seen what I have done in Egypt and you dwelt in the wilderness a long season.

Lamentations 3:43-44
Thou hast covered with anger and persecuted us; thou hast slain, thou hast not pitied. Thou hast **covered** thyself with a cloud, that our prayer should not pass through.

Deuteronomy 32:15
But Jeshurun waxed fat and kicked: thou art waxen fat, thou art grown thick, thou art **covered** with fatness; then he forsook God which made him and lightly esteemed the Rock of his salvation.

WHAT WE MUST COVER

Exodus 21:33-34
And if a man shall open a pit, or if a man shall dig a pit, and not **cover** it and an ox or an ass fall therein, the owner of the pit shall make it good and give money unto the owner of them and the dead beast shall be his.

Deuteronomy 23:13-14
And it shall be when thou wilt ease thyself abroad, thou shalt dig therewith and shalt turn back and **cover** that which comes from thee; For the Lord thy God walks in the midst of thy camp, to deliver thee and to give up thine enemies before thee; therefore, shall thy camp be holy; that he sees no unclean thing in thee, and turn away from thee.

Leviticus 17:13-14
And whatsoever man there be of the children of Israel or of the strangers that sojourn among you, which hunts and catches any beast or fowl that mat be eaten, he shall even pour out the blood thereof and **cover** it with dust. For it is the life of all flesh; the blood of it is for the life thereof; therefore, I said unto the children of Israel You shall eat the blood of no manner of flesh for the life of all flesh is the blood thereof: whosoever eats it shall be cut off.

Isaiah 58:7
Is it not to deal thy bread to the hungry and that thou bring the poor that are cast out to thy house? When thou sees the naked, that thou cover him; and that thou hide not thyself from thine own flesh?

I WANT TO BE A COVER GIRL

> **WHEN LOVE IS NOT THE COVERING** (Four examples of hatred stirring up strife)
>
> **Proverbs 10:12**
> Hatred stirs up strife; but love covers all sins.

Genesis 45:5-8 Joseph

And Joseph said unto his brethren, come near to me, I pray you. And they came near. And he said, I am Joseph your brother, whom you sold into Egypt. Now therefore be not grieved, nor angry with yourselves, that you sold me hither: for God did send me before you to preserve life. For these two years have the famine been in the land and yet there are five years, in which there shall neither be plowing nor harvest. And God sent me before you to preserve you a posterity in the earth, and to save your lives by a great deliverance. So now it was not you that sent me here, but God…Moreover he kissed all his brethren, and wept upon them: and after that his brethren talked with him. Joseph told them, "But as for you, you thought evil against me; but God meant it unto good, to bring to pass, as it is this day, to save much people alive."

1 Samuel 18:28/24:10-19 David

Saul became jealous and afraid of one that he had once loved greatly who had even become his armorbearer. For many years, he chased after David trying to kill him, but David honored the anointing upon the king and saved him. He had ample opportunities to return the favor to his enemy but he would not. David even killed the one who slew Saul at Saul's request. He questioned the man about his audacity to do it without fear.

I WANT TO BE A COVER GIRL

Matthew 26:4/John 20-21   Jesus Christ

When the chief priests, the scribes, and the elders assembled before the high priest Caiaphas, consulting to trick and kill Jesus, a woman having an alabaster box of very precious ointment poured it on his head. The disciples were concerned about its value and what other things could be done with it for the poor. They did not understand the covering this woman provided in anointing Jesus' body for burying.

Philemon 9:21   Paul

Paul was a prisoner of Jesus Christ and Onesimus was a prisoner in bonds. He became a prisoner of Jesus Christ also. Paul writes to fellow-laborers requesting them to receive Onesimus in the same manner they receive him. He goes on to say to them, "if you count me a partner, receive him as myself – if he has wronged you or owe you aught, put that on mine account – refresh my bowels in the Lord." Paul covered Onesimus.

> **WHEN LOVE IS NOT THE COVERING (Four examples of a fool's wrath)**
>
> **Proverbs 12:16**
> A fool's wrath is presently known; but a prudent man covers shame.

- **2 Kings 6:31** <u>Jehoram</u>

The king became desperate and wanted to take vengeance on the prophet Elisha. Like many ungodly men, he blamed a man of God for his troubles. Elisha's gift of discernment showed him what was to take place. God covered him.

- **1 King 19:1-2** <u>Jezebel</u>

Ahab reported to Jezebel about the prophets of Baal being destroyed. She became determined to destroy the man who had caused her idol god to be so humbled. She swore that by the next day Elijah would be dead like the prophets of Baal. She told Elijah of her intentions. He had the opportunity to escape. God covered him.

- **Daniel 3:19** <u>Nebuchadnezzar</u>

He was raged, hasty and angry with the three Hebrews that would not bow to his god and had them thrown into a furnace. They were confident that God would deliver them. They did not fear what the king so ordered. They stood their ground. God covered them.

- **Luke 4:16-31** <u>Men in Nazareth</u>

Men in Nazareth heard Jesus' sermon and were filled with wrath. They rose up to thrust Him out of the city, desiring to cast him down, but Jesus passing through them went his way. God covered him.

I WANT TO BE A COVER GIRL

> **WHEN LOVE IS THE COVERING (Five examples of Prudent men)**
>
> **Proverbs 13:16**
> In everything the prudent acts with knowledge, but a fool flaunts his folly.

Judges 8:2-3   **Gideon**

He had wisdom enough to pacify the anger of those who found fault or criticized.

1 Samuel 10:27   **Saul**

He held his peace when despised by the children of Belial.

Job 1:21-22   **Job**

Job denied covering up his sin as Adam did. In all Job did not sin nor charge God with wrong.

1 Samuel 17:29-30   **David**

David gave his resume which proved that he was able to stand against the Philistine.

Isaiah 36:21   **Hezekiah**

He held his peace at the king's commandment as the king compared his gods to Hezekiah's God; but Hezekiah knew that His God was God and was able to deliver.

I WANT TO BE A COVER GIRL

> **Proverbs 17:9** He that covers a transgression seeks love; but he that repeats a matter separates very friends. He that covers up and seeks to hide from others the faults and sins of a friend seeks his peace and love, but he that seeks to expose brings bitterness, hatred and equity between the best of friends.
>
> **Proverbs 28:13** He who covers his sins will not prosper, but whoever confesses and forsakes them will have mercy.

Three Examples of Men Covering Their Sins:

Genesis 3:12/Job 31:33	Adam	The woman who you gave me…. If I cover my iniquity as Adam…
Genesis 4:9	Cain	Where is Abel thy brother? Am I my brother's keeper?
1 Samuel 15:18-21	Saul	And Saul said unto Samuel, Yes, I have obeyed the voice of the Lord and have gone the way which the Lord sent me, and have brought Agag the king of Amalek, and have utterly destroyed the Amalekites.

I WANT TO BE A COVER GIRL

LOVE'S COVERING:

1 Peter 4:8

And above all things have fervent love for one another, for "love will cover a multitude of sins."

James 5:19-20

Brethren, if anyone among you wanders from the truth, and someone turns him back, let him know that he who turns a sinner from the error of his way will save a soul from death and cover a multitude of sins.

Ezekiel 28:12-19

The king of Tyrus was covered with every precious stone and he was the covering cherub. His heart was lifted up because of his beauty so he was exposed and could no longer be covered by the creator.

Romans 4:7

Blessed are they whose iniquities are forgiven, and whose sins are covered.

Matthew 10:26

Fear them not therefore, for there is nothing covered that shall not be revealed; and hid, that shall not be known.

Isaiah 60:2

For behold the darkness shall cover the earth and gross darkness the people, but the Lord shall arise upon thee and his glory shall be seen upon thee.

I WANT TO BE A COVER GIRL

1 Corinthians 11:7

For a man indeed ought not to cover his head, forasmuch as he is the image and glory of God: but the woman is the glory of the man.

Luke 23:30

Then shall they begin to say to the mountains, Fall on us, and to the hills, cover us.

I WANT TO BE A COVER GIRL

 I want to Connect with you

 I want to Lift you up

 I want to Agree with you

 I want to Unite with you

Victoria R. Bradley

I WANT TO BE A COVER GIRL

I want to Bridge the gap

I want to Cover you in the good times

I want to Cover you in the bad times

I want to Help you stay full
and never reach empty

I want to Embrace you when you
are hurting

Like the farmer (representing God) in the picture is covering everything, we need to cover our fellowmen in the same manner - that's

L   O   V   E

We, as people, need to cover one another's nakedness (weaknesses, short falls), just as God covers our nakedness. We all need covering from time to time. But we can't do it without a heart of love and we can't love each other unless we love God first. First things first.

Love is the cover we need to use. God is LOVE. If we would just stand still and see the salvation of the Lord – and see others through the eyes of God. If we would just put ourselves in the place that we find others in, we could easily cover them.

No more pointing the finger at another. No more gossiping and backbiting or sowing discord among one another. No more looking down on one another.

We spend so much time coming against each other, that we lose sight of who the real enemy is. We are to come against the enemy together, as one man (in the spirit).

If we refuse to walk in "love", we cannot cover others. Love is the ultimate thing and is the ultimate weapon against the enemy. First Corinthians 13 speaks to us about that "agape" love; that love that is active "in spite of," not "because of."

GOD IS OUR ULTIMATE COVERING FOR HE IS LOVE!

We are supposed to reflect HIM!

LOVE IS THE BLANKET THAT COVERS

OUTLOOK OF THE WRITER

In this book, the Lord allowed me to share a bit of the many experiences I've had in my life. The journey was quite rough at times because of my ignorance of the Word and Promises of God. As I grew up in Him, the roughness of the journey became smoother. The Lord allowed me to share about the things that I thought were sent by the enemy to distract, hinder, or paralyze me. When, in fact, He orchestrated every detail so that I could become on the outside what He had processed on the inside.

None of those "things" changed the mind of God concerning me. I am still who He says I am. I can do all things that He says I can, and I have everything that He has ordained for me to have. In spite of every challenge, I still stand because of God's grace and mercy. It took all the integers to make me who I am. It's called process.

I can look back at the past and see the teacher. I now live in the NOW.

ABOUT THE AUTHOR

Victoria R. Bradley is a mother and grandmother. She is retired from the U.S. Air Force and is now in full time work in the Kingdom of God.

She is the daughter of the late Barbara J. Pierce and the late Frazier Mitchell. She was brought up in the home of her late grandparents, James and Mary Ragins, who lived in Williamsburg County, South Carolina.

Never in a million years did she think she would be writing anything, but as the Lord led, she has put her pen to paper.

PRAYER

Father, in the name of Jesus,

As you instructed me to write these things, I know that you have an audience of sons and daughters who need to read what I have written...the pages of my life that you've allowed me to share.

I thank you for those who will be impacted, inspired, and invoked by this book.

The journey has been just that and I have only you to thank for my yet being here at this time. I thank you for your grace and your mercy. And, I thank you for the destiny and purpose you have ordained for our lives.

AMEN

"This book is inspiring! What truly caught my attention were the lessons Victoria learned. It's one thing to live but if we never learn anything from living, it would be in vain. From reading about the lessons and the different ways she now views life, many should be able to identify with her. Everything that looks bad is not always bad. It just depends on how you look at it. After reading this, you will be encouraged to continue to pray, to stand, and to hold on to God's unchanging hand. Thanks for your words of encouragement that were birthed out of your discouragement."

Eleanor Pressley

"It's amazing what we are able to see if we take the time to reflect, reminisce, and review our actions and responses in life. After reading the book, I hear another testimony, along with my own, of life and how it affects us in different ways. We can overcome so much if we can see the glass half full rather than see it half empty. I heard that somewhere. "

Jackie Garland

"Girl, I never knew you had all of this on the inside of you. I'm excited for the mere fact that our paths have crossed. I have a better understanding of who you are. Thanks for sharing with us the different ways of looking at life as you have experienced. Continue, my sister, continue."

Donna Taylor

www.ingramcontent.com/pod-product-compliance
Lightning Source LLC
Chambersburg PA
CBHW081408080526
44589CB00016B/2502